DESTOCKING IN THE RECESSION

Destocking in the Recession

CLIFF PRATTEN
Senior Research Officer
Department of Applied Economics
University of Cambridge

Gower

Published by
Gower Publishing Company Limited,
Gower House, Croft Road, Aldershot, Hants GU11 3HR, England

and

Gower Publishing Company,
Old Post Road, Brookfield, Vermont 05036, U.S.A.

British Library Cataloguing in Publication Data

Pratten, C.F.
Destocking in the recession.
1. Depressions 2. Great Britain——Industries
3. Great Britain——Economic condition——1945-
I. Title
338.5'42'0941 HC256.6

ISBN 0-566-00834-3

Library of Congress Cataloging in Publication Data

Pratten, C.F. (Clifford Frederick)
Destocking in the recession.

1. Inventories--Great Britain. 2. Industrial management--Great Britain. 3. Great Britain--Economic conditions--1945- . I. Title
HC260.I6P73 1985 338'.06 84-27886

ISBN 0-566-00834-3

Printed and bound in Great Britain by
Biddles Ltd, Guildford and Kings Lynn.

Contents

Preface

The study described in this paper was initiated by the Department of Applied Economics in 1981 to assess the importance of destocking for the 1979/81 recession, and to discover the reasons for the destocking. Completion of the study was made possible by a grant from the Department of Industry. Mr N.G. Attenborough and Mr D.A. Russell, Economic Advisers at the Department of Industry, made many helpful comments on drafts of the paper and Mr R.I. Armitage of the Central Statistical Office provided suggestions and data for Chapter 1. However the views expressed in the paper are those of the author, and are not attributable to the Department of Industry.

Evidence about the causes of destocking was obtained from managers of companies in answers to questions at interviews. I am particularly grateful for their cooperation.

Professor W.B. Reddaway provided advice when the study was at the planning stage. The Director of the Department, Mr Wynne Godley, read the draft manuscript and made many constructive comments relating to Chapters 5 and 7. Mr B.M. Deakin and Mr M. Landesmann also provided helpful comments on drafts of the paper.

Introduction

The reduction in the output of UK manufacturing industries in 1980 and 1981 was the most rapid on record. It is clear that a cause of the reduction in output was destocking by manufacturers, retailers and distributors. The main purpose of the project of research described in this paper was to find the reasons for this destocking, in order to improve understanding of how the economy operates and methods of forecasting.

The study records some of the responses of managers and firms to the 1980/81 recession and intense financial pressures. The results of the study have implications for other decisions made by managers and decision making in other sectors of the economy in response to shocks. For example, many companies reduced employment as well as stocks, and many households faced similar problems in 1980 and 1981. Explanations for the changes in stocks are also needed for understanding the effects of the economic policies introduced by Mrs Thatcher's government in 1979.

The novel approach to tracing the causes of destocking was to find the reasons why individual companies reduced their stocks. Managers of a sample of fifty companies, who agreed to co-operate, were asked to provide data showing changes in their companies' stocks to sales ratios and to describe the reasons for changes in the stocks held by their companies.

A referee of the original proposal to study the reasons for changes in stocks in 1980 and 1981 argued that 'attitudes to stocks may differ at different management levels' and that it would 'be sensible .... to investigate a few large companies in depth in order to gain an appreciation of the complexities of the problem - in particular, the numerous and complex strategic and operating considerations contributing to the decision to reduce stock levels'. The referee could have added different management functions, finance, production and marketing, to 'levels'. The approach suggested by the referee would produce interesting results, but in 1981 many companies were facing intense pressure from the fall in demand, the high exchange rate and high interest rates. It was unrealistic to expect them to allow 'in depth' studies of stockholding, involving many interviews at different levels of management. Contrary to the referee's view, the senior managers of many companies made deliberate decisions to reduce stocks in 1980 and 1981 and knew the reasons for the changes in their companies' stocks. Destocking did not emerge from a large number of independent decisions made at different levels of management. Also, the approach adopted was cost efficient, and there was a good chance of getting interesting and useful results from it.

Although destocking was discussed with only one or a small number of managers at each company, taking the sample as a whole, managers at different levels and with different responsibilities were included in the discussions, but there was a strong bias towards managers with responsibility for finance. A description of the responsibilities of the managers is given in Appendix A.

Managers knew the pressures which had caused them to destock, but there were many pressures operating simultaneously. No single device for assessing the relative importance of the different pressures was developed, but a lot of evidence on the causes of destocking was obtained during discussions with managers and by analyses of data published in company accounts and official sources. This evidence is used to assess the relative importance of the pressures for destocking.

Contents

The importance of stocks and changes in stocks for the economy are described in Chapter 1 and the economic scene during the period of destocking is outlined in Chapter 2. The contribution of destocking to the recession is assessed in Chapter 3. The factors determining changes in levels of stocks and the relevant economic theories are reviewed in Chapter 4.

Stock relief enabled firms to deduct increases in the value of their stocks from profits assessable to tax and influenced some decisions about stockbuilding and destocking. The rules for stock relief are described in Chapter 5. One focus of the enquiry was to trace changes in the ratios of stocks to output and sales. In Chapter 6 movements of these ratios for the manufacturing and retail sectors are described. The financial record of the sample of companies which destocked is described in Chapter 7. Chapter 8 records the information about the causes of destocking which was obtained from this sample of companies. Chapter 9 summarises the evidence obtained from a sample of companies which did not destock. The information reported in Chapters 8 and 9 provides material for the assessment of the relative importance of the factors causing destocking made in Chapter 10. The results of the study are summarised in Chapter 11.

1 The importance of stocks

Total stocks held in the economy are related to other economic variables, and the contribution of changes in stocks to movements in aggregate demand and output are described in this Chapter. Stocks are defined for National Income purposes as 'assets for use in future production, which can be used only once, and goods awaiting purchase which constitute stocks and work in progress... partly finished products awaiting completion in factories'. [1]

STOCKS HELD AT THE END OF 1979

Estimates of stocks are obtained from national income accounts. The Central Statistical Office (CSO) believes its estimates of the levels of stocks and the movements of stocks to be among the least accurate of the national income statistics. Table 1.1 shows the stocks held at the end of 1979 at 'recorded book prices'. Recorded book prices are the values of stocks held as recorded by firms. Book values are usually measured at historic purchase prices. The average rate at which stocks turnover is usually fairly rapid, so historic prices are similar to, but not precisely the same as, current prices. [2]

Total stocks of all types held by enterprises at the end of 1979 were valued at £67 billion, and stocks held in manufacturing industries represented 52 per cent of the total. Stocks held by retailers, the other main sector included in the industrial enquiry, were 12 per cent of total stocks, and the two sectors together accounted for 64 per cent of estimated total stocks. The table also shows the division of manufacturing stocks between raw materials, work in progress and finished goods.

Table 1.1
Stocks at the end of 1979

	£ billion	Percentage at total
Total Stocks and Work in Progress	66.7	100
of which:		
Manufacturing	34.4	52
of which:		
Raw materials	12.1	(18)
Work in progress	12.3	(18)
Finished goods	10.0	(15)
Retail distribution	8.3	12
Wholesale distribution	12.3	18
Other Sectors	11.7	18

Source: National Income and Expenditure 1983 Edition and MDS October, 1983.

The most reliable estimates of stocks are those for manufacturing. Quarterly surveys made by the Business Statistics Office (BSO) cover about 50 per cent of manufacturers' stocks. Grossed up estimates from these surveys are subsequently revised using data from annual Censuses of Production which have more comprehensive coverage. Surveys of retailers' and wholesalers' stocks are also made quarterly, and the results are revised using annual BSO enquiry data. The sample coverages of distributive trade surveys and enquiries are lower than for manufacturing. Estimates of stocks held in the service industries are least reliable. Stockholding in parts of the service sector (for example the motor trades and catering) is not surveyed between annual enquiries. Some service industries (including professional and scientific services, insurance, banking and finance, and private sector transport), in which absolute levels and changes in stocks are probably relatively small, are not covered at all in the national income series. Estimates of stock levels are therefore more likely to be under than over stated. [3]

Table 1.2 relates stocks to other economic aggregates. For the economy as a whole the value of stocks held at the end of 1979 represented 39 per cent of the annual flow of output measured by GDP in 1979. Stocks include imported goods held in stock while GDP excludes imports, so a more meaningful

Table 1.2
Stocks in Relation to Other Economic Aggregates
at the end of 1979

	Whole Economy	of which Manufacturing	Retailing	Other Sectors
	£ billion			
	(The figures in brackets are percentages of data for the whole economy)			
Stocks held at the end of 1979 at recorded book prices	66.7	34.4 (52)	8.3 (12)	24.0 (36)
Stocks of Fixed Assets held at the end of 1979 [a]	617.3	116.7 (19)	500.6 (81)	
GDP in 1979 at average 1979 factor cost	169.1	47.8 (28)	121.3 (72)	
Total Final Expenditure in 1979 at average 1979 factor cost	223.6	n.a.	n.a.	
Sales in 1979	n.a.	147.5	51.5	n.a.

[a] Net of depreciation and at current replacement cost.

Source: National Income and Expenditure 1983 Edition and the CSO.

comparison for the economy is stocks to total final expenditure, the output of the economy before deducting the import content of that output. Stocks represented thirty per cent of total final expenditure in 1979. Stocks held by manufacturing industries were valued at 72 per cent of their net output, and stocks held in the rest of the economy (including retailing) represented 27 per cent of its net output. [4] Manufacturing industries have a higher ratio of stocks to output than the rest of the economy (taken together). If stocks change in proportion to changes in output, then a fall in output of the manufacturing sector will result in more destocking than would a fall in output of the other sectors.

Stocks can be compared to inventories of other assets. For the whole economy, stocks were valued at 10.8 per cent of the net stock of fixed assets in 1979, and for manufacturing 29 per cent.

The ratio of stocks to sales is the basis for economic analysis of stocks and is used by managers as a guide for monitoring and controlling stocks. For manufacturing industries the overall ratio of stocks at the end of 1979 to sales during 1979, was 0.23 and for retailing 0.16. [5]

STOCKBUILDING

So far the level of stocks in 1979 has been described. Net stockbuilding, the increase in physical stocks, is now considered. Stockbuilding during the 1970's is shown in Table 1.3. To calculate the change in the volume of stocks - stockbuilding - stocks are revalued at average 1980 prices, not at recorded prices as in Tables 1.1 and 1.2. Apart from the different price valuation, the coverage of the figures in Table 1.3 is restricted to the value of the physical increase of stocks (i.e. stock appreciation - which reflects increases in prices - would be included in changes between successive book value levels as shown in Tables 1.1 and 1.2, but is excluded in Table 1.3).

As the correct figures for stockbuilding are not known, errors cannot be estimated. The CSO's assessment is that the errors in estimates of the annual change in the volume of stocks may be as high as half a per cent of GDP. Errors in the quarterly estimates (particularly recent quarters not yet covered in annual enquiries) are larger still.

Table 1.3
Stockbuilding during the 1970's at 1980 market prices

	Value of physical increase in stocks and work in progress			Year to year change in stock building shown in column(1)[a]	
	(1)	(2)	(3)	(4)	(5)
	£ million	as % of GDP	as % of total final expenditure	£ million	as % of GDP
1971	533	0.3	0.2	-	-
1972	-22	0.0	0.0	-555	-0.3
1973	5,047	2.4	1.9	+5,069	+2.3
1974	2,860	1.3	1.1	-2,187	-1.0
1975	-2,901	-1.4	-1.1	-5,761	-2.7
1976	1,081	0.5	0.4	+3,982	+1.8
1977	2,638	1.2	1.0	+1,557	+0.7
1978	2,090	0.9	0.7	-548	-0.2
1979	2,490	1.1	0.9	+400	+0.2
1980	-3,236	-1.4	-1.1	-5,726	-2.5
1981	-2,655	-1.2	-0.9	+581	+0.3
1982	-1,031	-0.4	-0.4	+1,624	+0.7
Average	575	0.3	0.2	-216	-0.1
Modulus	-	1.0	0.8	-	1.1

[a] Stockbuilding includes changes in work in progress
Source: National Income and Expenditure 1983.

The estimates of stockbuilding are occasionally adjusted to reconcile the estimates of GDP based on expenditure data with the estimates of GDP based on output and income data. For example, if the estimates of the increase in GDP based on output and income data exceed that based on expenditure data, the estimate of stockbuilding may be raised to increase the expenditure estimate of GDP. Such adjustments are included in the estimates of changes in the stocks of 'other industries', though the need for them may be faulty recording of stockbuilding elsewhere in the economy, or of other components of expenditure altogether. Usually it has been found that these adjustments can be removed after expenditure data from benchmark inquiries and more reliable income data become available. [6]

The data in Table 1.3 show that on average stockbuilding has represented a small part of aggregate demand, only 0.2 per cent of total final expenditure, or 0.3 per cent of GDP, between 1971 and 1982, but it is the most volatile component and has significant impact on year to year changes in aggregate demand. The year to year changes in stocks averaged 1.1 per cent of GDP during the twelve years to 1982, and the swing from stockbuilding in 1979 to destocking in 1980 represented as much as 2.5 per cent of GDP. However these comparisons exaggerate the effects of changes in stockbuilding because there are compensating changes in imports; if stockbuilding increases, imports increase.

The impact of stockbuilding on the output of the economy depends upon whether changes in stocks reinforce or offset changes in other components of demand and supply. A method of illustrating the effects of changes in stocks on the growth of output is to compare the growth of output including, and excluding, stockbuilding net of imports as in Diagram 1.1. Imports were assumed to account for a steady fifty per cent of stockbuilding for this exercise. [7] The comparison is artificial in the sense that if stockbuilding had been zero - the implied position when stockbuilding is excluded from GDP - then other components of aggregate demand and supply would have been different. For example, there are some multiplier effects of stockbuilding, so lower stockbuilding would lead to lower consumers' expenditure. Also a rise in stocks may be involuntary rather than a deliberate increase; it may be caused by disappointed expectations of a rise in demand from consumers. However these qualifications should not be allowed to obscure the clear message of Diagram 1.1, that changes in stocks have not been a very powerful factor, and certainly not a dominant factor, causing fluctuations in the growth of output. (The coefficient of variation was reduced by 14 per cent by the exclusion of stockbuilding). In 1973 and 1976 stockbuilding, and in 1980 destocking, increased the amplitude of changes in GDP, but changes in stocks have not done this consistently.

Diagram 1.1 GDP (Y) and GDP minus Stockbuilding (Y-S)
Percentage changes compared to the same quarter of the previous year.

	Mean	S.D.	Coeff. of Var.
Y	2.34	2.58	1.098
Y-S	2.35	2.21	0.942

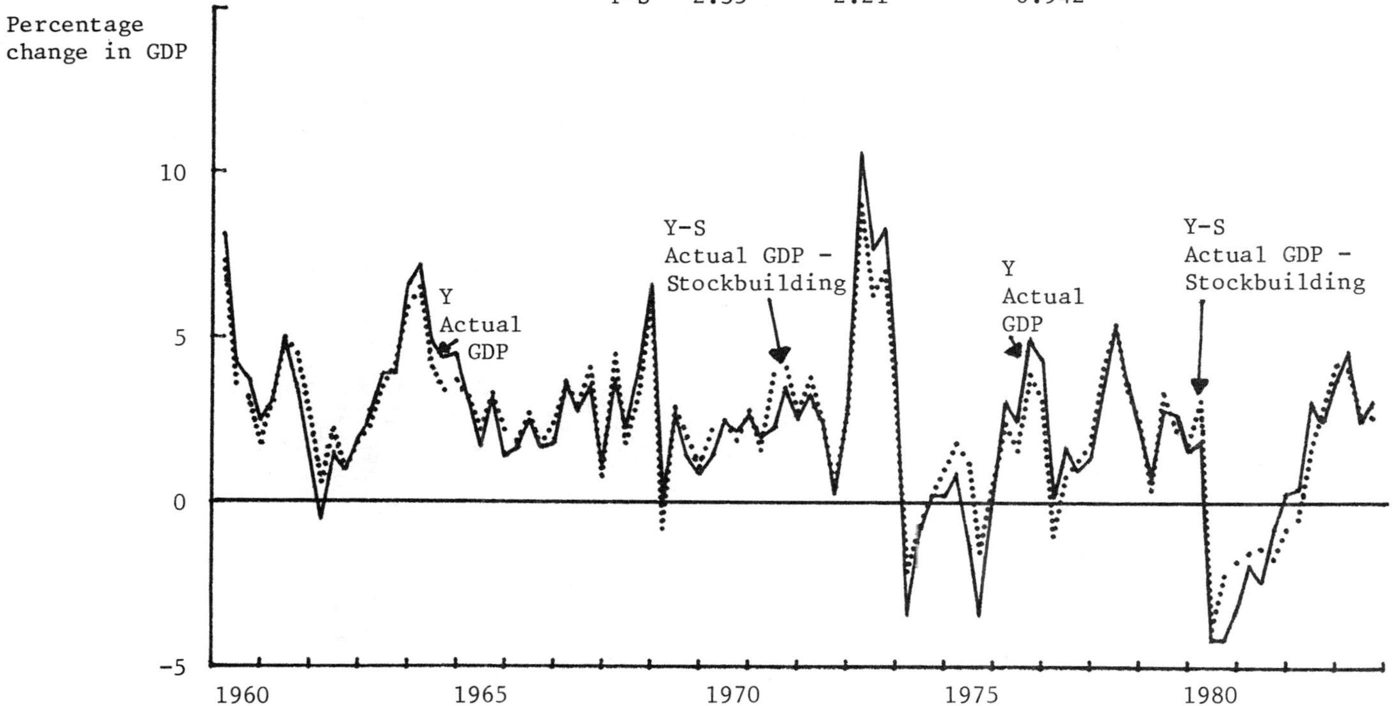

Source: ETAS 1984 and Economic Trends December 1983.

NOTES

[1] R. Maurice, '<u>National Accounts Statistics Sources and Methods</u>', London, 1968.

[2] Wholesale price indices rose between 30th September 1979 (a representative date for the purchase of stocks held at the year end) and the end of 1979. The wholesale price index for the output of manufacturing industries rose by four per cent, and for materials and fuel purchased by manufacturing industries by nine per cent.

[3] Growing timber, which cannot be increased in volume terms other than by new planting and slow natural growth, is included in the estimates for 'other sectors'. At the end of 1979 the book value of forestry industry stocks was £1.3 billion.

[4] Net output is output net of inputs bought from other sectors, but before any deduction for capital consumption.

[5] The reciprocal of the stocks to sales ratio, the average number of times stocks are turned over per year, was four for manufacturing and six for retailing. A third way of describing these relationships is in terms of 'pipelines'. Manufacturing stocks at cost represent twelve weeks, and retail stocks eight weeks, sales. These measures of stock turnover and pipelines are qualified by the valuation of stocks which are at cost not selling prices. The average length of time goods are in stock is longer than indicated.

[6] A special adjustment was made for the 1981 Blue Book estimate of stockbuilding in 1979. The value of the physical increase in stocks was adjusted upwards by £1 billion at current prices, three per cent of stocks, 'in the light of the imbalance between the income and expenditure estimates of GDP.'

[7] The percentage import content of changes in stocks was 45 per cent according to the Input-Output tables for 1974. In practice the percentage must have increased during the period from 1960 to 1982, as import penetration increased generally, and varied from quarter to quarter with changes in the composition of changes in stocks.

2 The economic scene 1979-82

Between 1979 and 1982 the British economy was characterised by falling output, rising then falling inflation and a doubling of the level of unemployment to 12 per cent. Indices of output according to the three methods of estimation are shown in Diagram 2.1. The 'expenditure' estimates show a fall of 4.9 per cent between the average for the first three quarters of 1979 and the second quarter of 1981, while the 'output' data indicate a slightly sharper decline of 5.5 per cent over the same period. [1] The recession was concentrated on the industrial sector; the index of industrial production fell by 10.9 per cent and that for manufacturing production by 15.4 per cent.

The roots of this sharp slump lie in the events of the early and mid-1970's. The Heath government used expansive fiscal and monetary policies in 1972 and 1973 to increase output. Output did increase sharply but so did the rate of inflation. In the aftermath of the oil price rise in 1973 and 1974, world and UK industrial output fell in 1974 and 1975. The British economy did not fully recover from this downturn; unemployment continued at post-war record levels and rapid inflation persisted. A major factor inhibiting recovery was the pervasive world recession, but it is evident from Table 2.1 that from 1979 Britain endured an industrial recession markedly more severe than, for example, Germany or France. It is with an outline of its causes that the remainder of this chapter will be concerned.

Diagram 2.1 Indices of GDP at 1980 prices
(Average first three quarters of 1979 = 100)

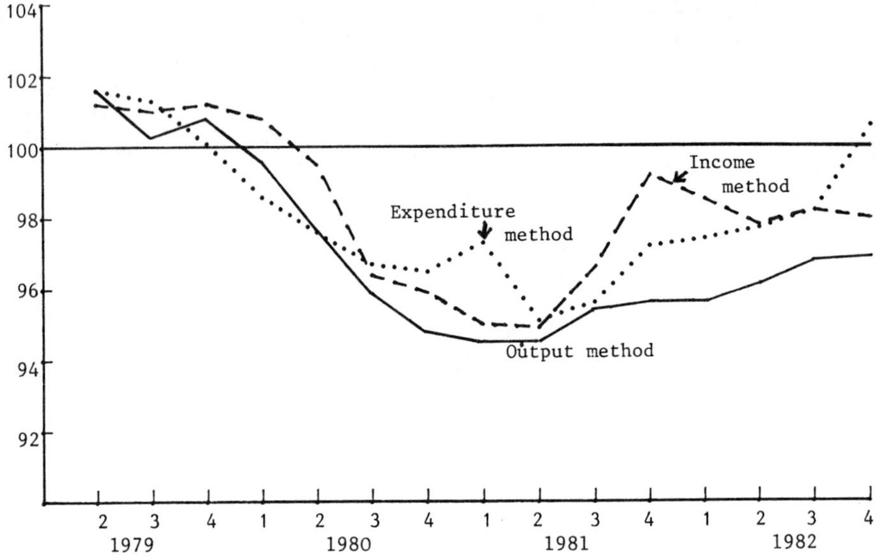

Diagram 2.2 Growth of the Real Money Supply £M_3 [a]
(Average for first three quarters of 1979 = 100)

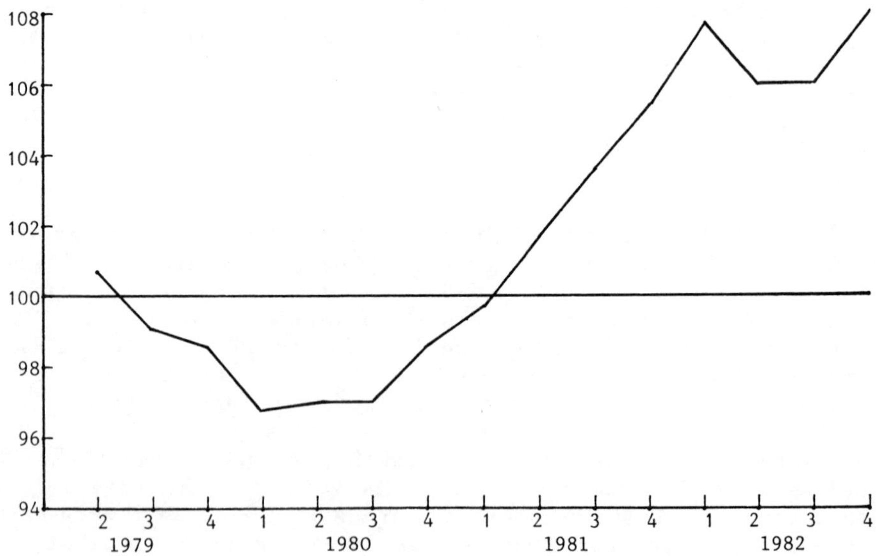

(a) A definition of the real money supply is given in the text.

Source: Economic Trends, October, 1983.

Table 2.1.

An International Comparison of Industrial Production and Unemployment. [a]

	Industrial Production (1975 = 100)				Percentage Unemployed			
	UK	USA	France	Germany	UK	USA	France	Germany
1975	100	100	100	100	4.7	8.3	4.1	3.6
1976	103	111	109	107	6.0	7.5	4.4	3.7
1977	108	117	110	110.5	6.3	6.9	4.7	3.6
1978	112	124	113	113	6.3	5.9	5.2	3.5
1979	116	129.5	118	117	5.6	5.7	5.9	3.2
1980	108.5	125	118	117	7.0	7.0	6.3	3.0
1981	104	128	117	116	10.7	7.5	7.3	4.4
1982	106	118	115	113	12.5	9.5	8.0	6.1

Sources: OECD. 'Main Economic Indicators', November 1983, and 1960-79, and 'Historical Statistics' 1960-81.

[a] The data are based on OECD definitions.

At the time the Conservatives came to power in May 1979, the economy was already struggling. GDP had increased by only eight per cent in six years from its previous peak in 1973. Productivity growth was slow, output per person had increased by 7.2 per cent over the same period. Inflation was a major problem, standing at an annual rate of 10.4 per cent in May 1979, with the prospect of further price rises due to the wage settlements secured during the 'Winter of Discontent' of 1978/9, and commitments to future rises agreed to at that time. From this situation, the economy sank into recession; real GDP fell, unemployment rose dramatically and inflation continued at rates of over 15 per cent until the end of 1980.

What were the immediate causes of the recession? The oil price shock in 1979 and 1980 triggered world recession. The soaring price of oil and the development of North Sea oil combined to force up the sterling exchange rate. In addition the Conservative government deliberately deflated the economy. Its express intention on its election was the reduction of inflation, and it was to this end that the medium term financial strategy was introduced in 1980. With monetarism as its theoretical base, the government attempted to reduce the rate of growth of the money supply by raising interest rates and by restricting public expenditure to cut the PSBR. Both measures had a deflationary impact on the economy. The sharp rise in interest rates is shown in Diagram 2.3. In 1980 the Treasury Bill rate rose to record levels and real interest rates measured by the yield on Treasury Bills adjusted by the change in consumer prices, were positive [2]. As a percentage of GDP, the PSBR fell from 6.5 per cent in 1979 to 4.25 per cent in 1981, but this understates the deflationary impact of the government's fiscal stance, since the recession itself was exerting upward pressure on the PSBR. The money supply as measured by real £M3 fell from the second quarter of 1979 until the second quarter of 1980, and only regained the second quarter 1979 level in the second quarter of 1981. (Diagram 2.2) [3] The government's fiscal and monetary policy deepened the recession at least in the short run.

A major focus of attention throughout the recession was the movement of the sterling exchange rate. From the last quarter of 1976, the exchange rate recovered and then shot upwards in 1979 and 1980 (Diagram 2.4). The rise in 1979 occurred despite a more rapid rate of inflation in Britain than was experienced by our principal competitors. The initial recovery of sterling from its trough in 1976 was based on North Sea oil prospects and was checked by the Labour government. The new Conservative government left the rate to adjust with market forces, which pushed it up in 1979. The main market forces causing the

Diagram 2.3 U.K. and U.S. Interest Rates[a]

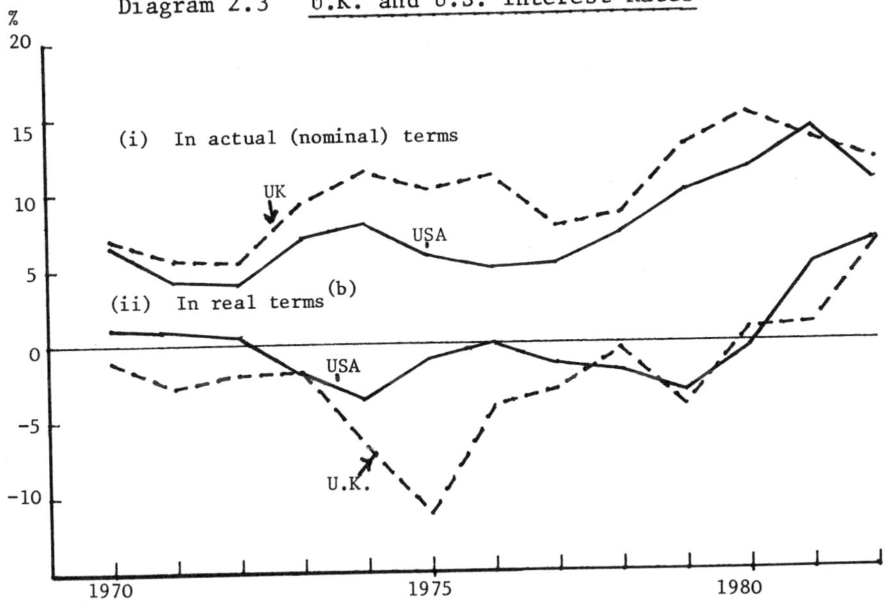

(a) Treasury bill rates.

(b) Real interest rates are defined in the text.

Diagram 2.4 Sterling Effective Exchange Rate and Relative Wholesale Prices (Q_2 1979=100)

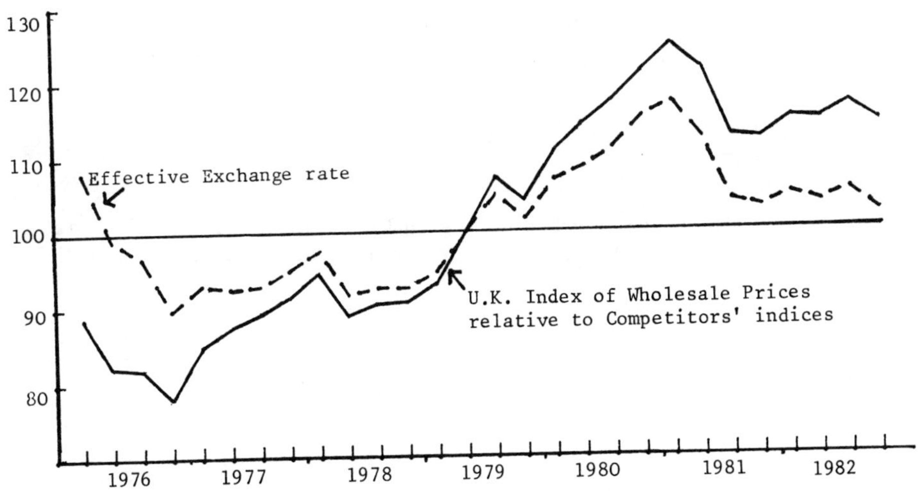

Sources: ETAS 84 and Survey of Current Business.

exchange rate to rise rapidly were the combined effects of the expansion of North Sea oil production on sterling, and the dampening effect of the oil price rise on foreign currencies. The government's contractionary monetary policy reinforced this pressure. Instead of reducing interest rates to moderate the rise or even devalue sterling, the government increased interest rates to deflate the economy and to hold down the growth of the money stock. American as well as British short-term interest rates are shown in Diagram 2.3. In 1981 a monetarist approach to economic policy operated in America as in Britain.

The remarkably sharp fall in British trade competitiveness measured by relative wholesale prices also shown in Diagram 2.4, was caused by the rising exchange rate combined with relatively rapid wage inflation in Britain. The declining competitiveness of British industry was a trigger for destocking - the subject of this paper. It was also the impetus behind the substantial increase in labour productivity during 1981 as firms struggled to recover their competitiveness.

The recession of 1980/81 originated in world recession and was compounded by the deflationary policy of the Conservative Government.

NOTES

[1] The CSO believe the output method to be the most reliable of the short term indicators of changes in output.

[2] Where the gross money yield on Treasury Bills for a year is x per cent, and the change in the retail price index between the beginning and end of the year is y per cent, the real interest rate is

$$\left(\left(\frac{100 + x}{100 + y} \times 100\right) - 100\right)$$

[3] The index of real money supply is an index of $£M_3$ as a percentage of the index of total home costs - the GDP deflator.

3 Destocking and the recession

DESTOCKING

The purpose of this chapter is to assess just how important destocking was as a source of falling demand in the 1980/81 recession, to see if there is any validity in the view that the recession of 1980/81 was a 'temporary aberration, the result of an unusually severe stock cycle,' [1] and to test 'whether destocking was the most important single element in the recession'. [2]

Table 3.1 shows the changes in stocks since the end of 1978, and Diagram 3.1 shows the data in percentage form. Stocks increased during 1979, then fell. Total stocks fell by 6.4 per cent in volume terms between the end of 1978 and the end of 1982, and in the manufacturing sector they fell by 12.5 per cent. The period of most intensive destocking was during the year from the end of June 1980. Total stocks fell by seven per cent, and destocking by manufacturing industries accounted for 69 per cent of the total. In marked contrast, retail stocks rose by six per cent between the end of 1978 and the end of 1982, though they fell sharply in the last quarter of 1979 and the first and last quarters of 1980; they fell by 5.7 per cent during 1980. [3]

Diagram 3.1 Movements of Stocks since 1979

(Stocks at the end of Q_4 1978=100)

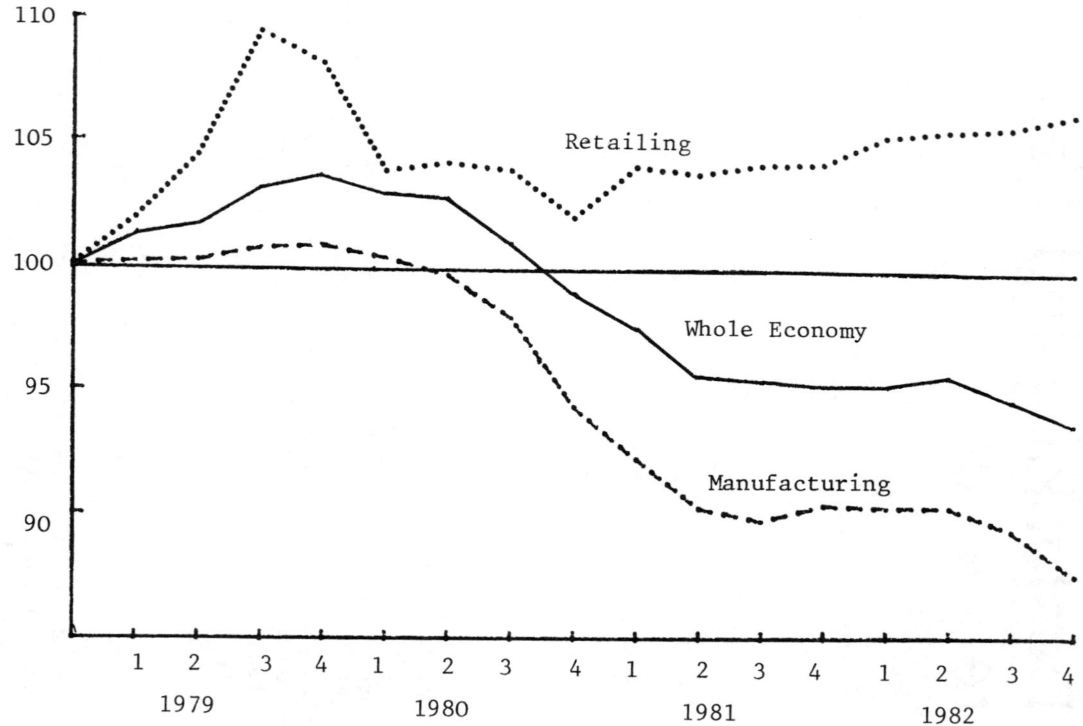

Source: Economic Trends December 1984

Stockbuilding was an important source of demand in the economy in 1979, helping to buoy it up. It became a significant source of deflation during 1980 and 1981.

Table 3.1
Changes in Stocks Since 1979

(£m at 1980 prices seasonally adjusted)

	Total		Manufacturing		Retailing		Other sectors	
Value of stocks end December 1978	(69,272)		(36,164)		(6,740)		(26,368)	
1979 Q1	+852		+45		+131		+676	
Q2	+279		+15		+168		+96	
Q3	+1040		+183		+336		+521	
Q4	+319		+32		-88		+375	
		+723		-200		-26		+949
1980 Q1	-501		-167		-292		-42	
Q2	-135		-248		+18		+95	
Q3	-1201		-636		-17		-548	
Q4	-1399		-1270		-127		-2	
		-4939		-3421		-28		-1490
1981 Q1	-1010		-762		+136		-384	
Q2	-1329		-753		-20		-556	
Q3	-182		-162		+22		-42	
Q4	-134		+219		+9		-362	
		-46		+25		+116		-187
1982 Q1	+27		-36		+74		-11	
Q2	+243		+4		+11		+228	
Q3	-621		-342		+9		-288	
Q4	-680		-634		+34		-80	

Source: Economic Trends, October 1983.

DESTOCKING AS A CAUSE OF THE RECESSION

(a) The no-change alternative

An emphasis on destocking as an explanation for the recession emerges from a comparison of the actual changes in stocks and output of the economy. The importance of changes in stocks are assessed in relation to a no-change alternative position - a stagnant economy in which there is no fall in output, but no growth either. This approach to assessing the recession was used by the Treasury in the 1981 Financial Statement.

Commenting on recent developments in the economy the Treasury stated 'the character of the recession, namely stable final demand, substantial destocking and a severe decline in manufacturing output, reflects the nature of the pressures on the company sector' [4].

A comparison of the first two rows of Table 3.2 demonstrates the importance of the turn round from stockbuilding in 1979 to destocking in 1981 when comparisons are made with the no-change alternative. The quarterly averages of GDP and the components of aggregate demand for the first three quarters of 1979 and the first two quarters of 1981 are shown in the first two rows, and the differences between them in row 3 [5]. These figures do seem to indicate the prime importance of the reduction in stocks as a source of recession. The fall in GDP over this period was £2,271 million, while the turn round from stockbuilding to destocking was £1,894 million. The other main changes were a fall in fixed investment and an improvement in the balance between exports and imports, as imports fell in part because of destocking. Also exports of oil increased and imports fell as North Sea oil production increased.

(b) <u>Three per cent Growth</u>

The no-change alternative position is not the only basis for assessing the importance of destocking in the recession. To gain a true impression of events in 1980 and 1981 it is useful to compare actual changes in stocks to the hypothetical movements of demand and output in a growing economy. For this purpose a growth rate of three per cent is used. Only growth at about this rate, however impracticable it may seem, prevents a further rise in unemployment; and it is from a comparison with this hypothetical alternative position, or a similar one, that the true sources of the recession can be assessed. [6]

Estimates of the change in GDP and stocks if the economy had grown at a steady three per cent per year are shown in Row 4 of Table 3.2. The increase in GDP at a quarterly rate between the first three quarters of 1979 and the first half of 1981 would have been £3,318 million. Assuming a constant stocks to output ratio, then stocks would have increased by three per cent a year in line with the hypothetical increase in output. On this basis stockbuilding in the first half of 1981 would have been £557 million a quarter, £167 million a quarter less than it averaged during the first three quarters of 1979. Row 5 shows the difference between actual output and the hypothetical output with three per cent growth. GDP was £5,589 million, 9.2 per cent below the level it would have reached in the first

Table 3.2. The Components of Aggregate Demand.
(£m at 1980 prices seasonally adjusted)

	GDP at market prices	Stocks	All other components of demand	Consumers' expenditure	Government consumption	Fixed investment	Exports	Imports
1. Actual average for:								
Q's 1, 2 and 3, 1979	58,205	724	57,481	34,398	11,894	10,350	15,672	14,834
Q's 1 and 2, 1981	55,394	-1,170	57,104	34,277	12,019	8,892	15,188	13,272
3. Change (2)-(1)	-2,271	-1,898	-377	-121	+125	-1,458	-484	-1,562
4. Hypothetical change if growth between the first three Q's of 1979 and the first two Q's of 1981 had been 3% p.a.	+3,318	-167	+3,485					
5. Difference between growth at 3% p.a. and actual change (3)-(4)	-5,589	-1,727	-3,862					
6. Adjustment for import content		863	-863					
7. Shortfall of demand compared to hypothetical growth of 3% p.a. (5)-(6)	-5,589	-864	-4,725					
(As percentage of reduction of GDP)	(100)	(15)	(85)					

Sources: Economic Trends October 1983 and assumptions described in the text.

half of 1981. The shortfall for stocks was £1,727 million and represented 31 per cent of the total.

These comparisons still exaggerate the importance of destocking for the output of the economy because stocks are the most import-intensive element of GDP. After excluding the estimated import content of the change in stocks in Row 7, the turn round from stockbuilding to destocking made up 15 per cent of the change in GDP. [7]

So far, the importance of destocking in the first half of 1981 has been described. The exercise was extended. Diagram 3.2 shows the deviations of GDP and stockbuilding from the three per cent growth trend for the period from the beginning of 1979 until the end of 1982. The three per cent trend growth of GDP was based on the actual average for the first three quarters of 1979. The deviations of stockbuilding from trend are the differences between actual stockbuilding and the level of stockbuilding with stocks increasing at three per cent a year taken as a percentage of GDP with growth of three per cent. Throughout the exercise it was assumed that the import content of stocks was 50 per cent, and that this applied to changes in stocks. In practice the effects of changes in stocks on imports must have varied from quarter to quarter depending upon the industrial distribution of changes in stocks and their division among categories of stocks.

By the second quarter of 1981, GDP was ten per cent below the level it would have reached with three per cent growth from the average of the first three quarters of 1979. The contribution of destocking to this relative fall in GDP was significant in 1980 and 1981, but it never rose above two per cent of GDP. Other factors taken together were clearly much more important than destocking. It is also evident from Diagram 3.2 that destocking was not the dominant factor at the start of the recession. These conclusions conform to the analysis shown in Diagram 1.1; changes in stocks are not the dominant factor causing changes in the growth of output of the economy.

Diagram 3.3 shows the deviations of actual GDP and stocks compared to the no-change alternative. The diagram shows the deviations of GDP and stocks as a percentage of GDP from the averages for the first three quarters of 1979. This comparison indicates that destocking in 1980 and 1981 compared to stockbuilding in 1979 was an important cause of the recession, but this is not a fair view of the importance of destocking. [8] Comparisons with the no-change alternative position has led to misleading conclusions about the sources of recession. [9]

Diagram 3.2 Deviations of GDP and Stockbuilding from 3% Growth Trend

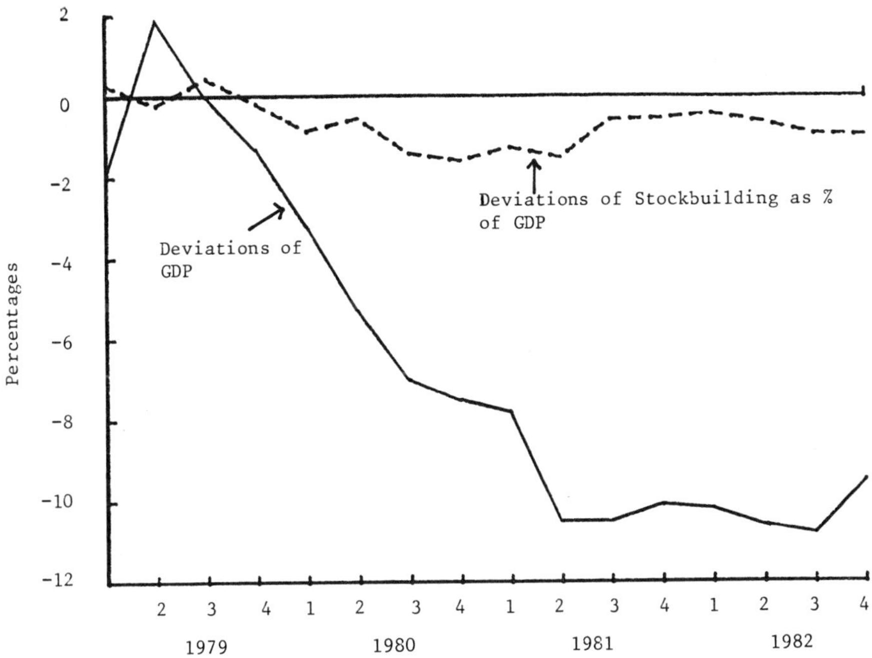

Diagram 3.3 Deviations from No-change Alternative Position

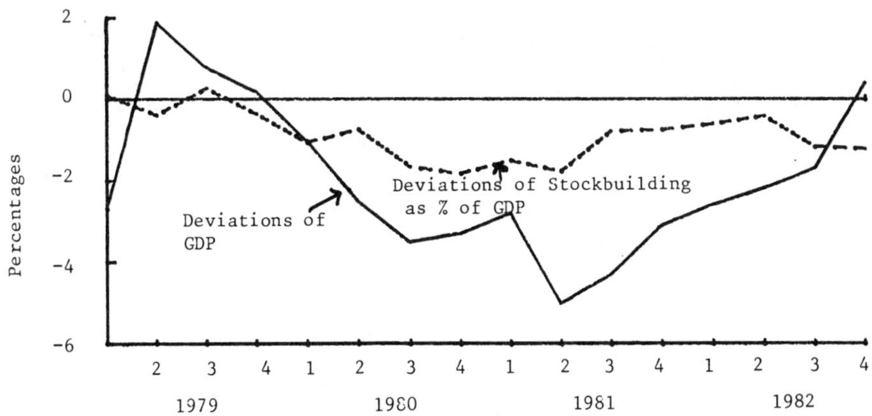

MANUFACTURING INDUSTRIES

The rather benign view of the recession indicated by Diagram 3.3 is misleading because the comparison is with a stagnant economy. It also hides the violent impact of the recession for many manufacturing industries. The extent of the recession varied markedly across industries; output of North Sea oil was rising, service industries were affected less than manufacturing industries, and the falls in output of the manufacturing industries producing food and electrical investment goods were relatively mild. The decline in output was concentrated on the other sectors of manufacturing. Some of these contrasts are shown in Table 3.3.

Table 3.3
An Industrial Profile of the Recession

	1979 to 1981	1979Q4 to 1980Q4
	Percentage Change	
GDP		
Expenditure method	-3.8	-3.6
Output method	-5.2	-6.0
	Percentage Change	
Volume of Retail Sales	+1.2	-0.9
Industrial Production	-10.2	-11.2
Manufacturing Production	-14.6	-15.5
Food, drink and tobacco	-3.3	-2.4
Chemicals and man made fibres	-10.3	-17.1
Metals	-19.2	-27.6
Engineering	-15.7	-15.7
of which electrical investment goods	-5.6	-4.1
Textiles, footwear and clothing	-22.4	-20.0

Sources: Monthly Digest of Statistics and Economic Trends, October 1983.

So far it has been shown that destocking was not a very important factor in the recession, and that the recession was concentrated on the manufacturing sector. This leaves the possibility that destocking was the cause of the steep decline in the output of manufacturing industries.

THE EFFECTS OF DESTOCKING FOR MANUFACTURING INDUSTRIES

The procedure used to estimate the effects of destocking on the output of manufacturing industries is described in the Appendix to this Chapter. The serious qualifications to the estimates which are described in the Appendix, mean that the results for any one quarter are not very reliable, but the estimates do provide an approximate guide over longer time spans. The results of the exercise, splitting changes in manufacturing output from the first quarter of 1979, between those attributable to stock changes and those caused by other changes, are shown in Diagram 3.4. These comparisons are on the same basis as those shown in Diagram 3.3, they are comparisons with a no-change alternative position and exaggerate the importance of destocking. On this basis destocking had as its counterpart a fall in the output of manufacturing industries of 3.9 per cent between the first three quarters of 1979 and the first half of 1981, while output fell by 15.6 per cent. Destocking accounted for less than a quarter of the decline. Again the conclusion is that destocking was not the dominant cause of the steep decline in the output of manufacturing industries.

CONCLUSIONS

It is apparent that destocking contributed to the recession, but the importance attached to destocking as a primary cause of recession was exaggerated because comparisons were made with a stagnant economy. The main conclusion is that the recession of 1980/1 was not the result of destocking alone; other deflationary factors were exerting a strong influence on the economy.

The conclusion is unsurprising, but it should not obscure the fact that destocking was for a time a component of the decline in the demand for the products of manufacturing industries. The high rate of destocking contributed to bankruptcies during 1980 and 1981 which increased unemployment. Although the significance of destocking as a causal factor in the recession should not be overstated, it was a factor aggravating a serious recession.

Diagram 3.4 The Effects of Destocking on the Output of Manufacturing Industries

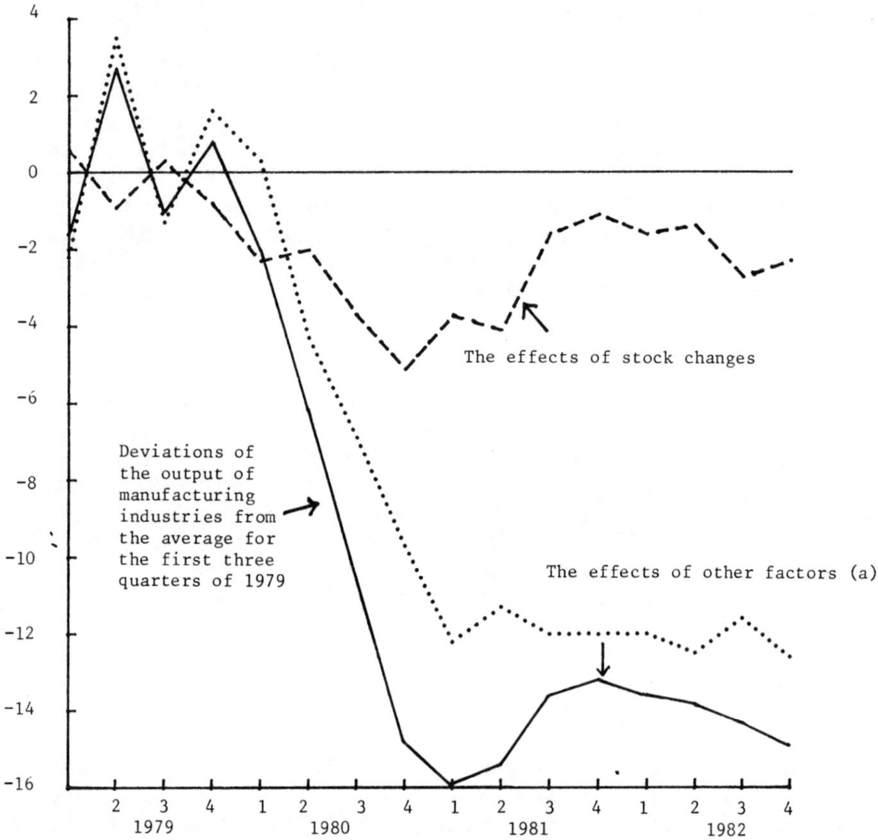

(a) Estimated as a residual between changes in manufacturing output and the effects of changes in stocks.

Appendix
The effects of stock changes on manufacturing output

This appendix describes a method of estimating the effects of stock changes on manufacturing output. The procedure involves distinguishing stocks of finished goods, work in progress and materials and fuel held by manufacturers. When a manufacturer reduces his stocks of finished goods and work in progress he cuts back his own output relative to sales. Destocking of all three categories involves a reduction in purchases from suppliers, including other manufacturers, and the suppliers must either reduce their output or increase their own stocks. Destocking of UK produced manufactures by retailers and customers of manufacturers in other sectors, causes a fall in sales for manufacturers and hence an increase in manufacturers' stock and/or a cut in their output. These effects are now estimated and combined. The main problem for estimating the impact on manufacturing output of destocking is to split the effects of changes in stocks between home manufacturing, other domestic producers and imports. The estimates of this division are no more than best guesses. The procedure used is illustrated by comparing data for the first three quarters of 1979 and the first two of 1981.

We start with the reduction in manufacturers' output attributable to the reduction in their own stocks. In the first two quarters of 1981, manufacturers' stocks of finished goods fell by £278 million (at 1980 prices seasonally adjusted) at a quarterly rate, and by £1112 million at an annual rate.

One third of this destocking is reckoned to represent a fall in the manufacturers' own output, so the output loss was £371 million at an annual rate. Similarly one fifth of the decline in work in progress is reckoned to represent changes in manufacturers' own output. Work in progress fell by £131m a quarter in the first two quarters of 1981, causing a reduction in the manufacturers' output of £105 million at an annual rate. Combining the two reductions in output gives an output loss attributable to manufacturers' own destocking of £476 million, equivalent to about 0.8 per cent of the net output of the manufacturing sector in 1979. Similar calculations for the first three quarters of 1979 show the average increase in manufacturers' own output component of their stockbuilding was £66 million. The turn round from stockbuilding to destocking was £542 million, or 0.95 per cent of manufacturing output in 1979.

Estimates of the other effects of changes in stocks on the output of manufacturing industries are shown in Table 3.A.I. To summarise, the decline in stocks in the first two quarters of 1981 reduced the output of manufacturing industries by a further £855 million, 1.5 per cent of manufacturing output, and the turn round from stockbuilding to destocking between the first three quarters of 1979 and the first two quarters of 1981, reduced the output of manufacturing industries by £1,704 million, representing 3.0 per cent of manufacturing output in 1979. The total effect of the turn round from stockbuilding to destocking was £2,246 million about four per cent of manufacturing output in 1979.

The exercise was replicated for the period from the beginning of 1979 until the end of 1982 and the results are shown in Diagram 3.4.

There are serious qualifications to these estimates of the effects of destocking on the output of manufacturing industries which have been made in this Appendix. The proportions of destocking accounted for by the net output of manufacturing industries are no more than guess estimates. As averages the figures are unlikely to be seriously inaccurate, but stock changes in a particular quarter may be concentrated on the products of, say, the engineering industries or commodities such as oil, and oil related products, and this could affect the proportions and the estimates of the effects of destocking on manufacturing industries.

The calculations are for all manufacturing industries, the effects of destocking may have been much more important for some individual manufacturing trades and firms.

Table 3.A.1 Destocking and the Output of Manufacturing Industries. (1980 prices)

Stocks held by	Proportion of a change in stocks reflecting a reduction in:		Stockbuilding Average first:		Effect on the Output of Manufacturing industries at annual rate. Average for first:		
	manufacturers' own output	the output of manufact-uring	three q's of 1979	two q's of 1981	three q's of 1979	two q's of 1981	turn round
					£m		
Manufacturing							
Finished goods	0.333		+63	-278	+84	-371	-455
Work in progress	0.2		-22	-131	-18	-105	-87
Manufacturers' own output content of stockbuilding					+66	-476	-542
Manufacturing		0.2	+65(a)	-639	+52	-511	-563
Distribution		0.3	+546	-87	+655	-104	-759
Energy and Water		0.05	-109	-32	-22	-6	+16
Other Sectors		0.2	+205	-293	+164	-234	-398
Other manufacturing content of stockbuilding					+849	-855	-1,704
Total					+915	-1,331	-2,246

(a) Excluding manufacturers' own content of stockbuilding. The average stockbuilding by manufacturing industries during the first three quarters of 1979 was £81 million, less manufacturers' own output, a quarter of £66 million; £16 million = £65 million.

NOTES

[1] Quotation from the London Business School's '<u>Economic Outlook</u>' June 1981 p. 14.

[2] Quotation from '<u>The National Institute Economic Review</u>', May 1981 p. 23.

[3] The 'expenditure' estimates of stock changes shown in Table 3.1 and Diagram 3.1 are provisional; this applies particularly to the estimates for 1982. In the previous chapter it was shown that the 'output' estimates of GDP indicate a somewhat larger decline in output than the 'expenditure' estimates, of which stock changes are a part. It is quite possible that a part of the disparity between the output and expenditure methods of GDP measurement is due to errors in estimates of stockbuilding. If this is so, the figures cited underestimate the extent of the destocking.

[4] Page 23.

[5] Data for the first three quarters of 1979 were averaged to even out the distortions caused by the steep increase in VAT in June 1979. Other events which caused distortions in 1979 were the road haulage dispute and interruption to exports to Iran and Nigeria. These events increased stocks during the first quarter of 1979. The trough of the recession was in the first two quarters of 1981 according to the 'output' estimates of GDP.

[6] Although three per cent was the average annual rate of growth of the economy during the 1960's, the rate of growth between 1973 and 1978 averaged 1.1 per cent a year, far less than the three per cent used for this exercise. However most forecasters saw this as a temporary deviation from trend rather than as a new long-term norm, and they were projecting substantial rates of growth at the end of 1978, prior to the second oil crisis. For example, the London Business School forecast growth of 2.4 per cent a year between 1978 and 1982. (London Business School, 'Economic Outlook' February 1979). They summarised their forecast by saying 'the prospects are that the next four years will be considerably better than the last four with faster growth of output...' The hypothetical alternative position could be based upon a slower rate of growth than three per cent to reflect the slow down in growth in other industrial countries. Another possibility would be a comparison with the hypothetical position if the government had adopted different, more expansionary, policies; a drawback to this approach is that the effects of alternative policies are uncertain.

[7] The import content of stocks was estimated to be 50 per cent. Footnote (7) page eight gives the reasons for using this figure.

[8] If a hypothetical growth rate lower than three per cent had been used, this would have boosted the apparent importance of destocking in the recession towards that shown for the no-change comparison.

[9] Another reason why destocking may have been given more emphasis as a cause of the recession than our analysis attributes to it, is that the initial estimates of destocking have been scaled down. The revisions to the estimates of stockbuilding are shown in Table 3.4.

Table 3.4
Revisions to Estimates of Destocking

Changes in Stocks at 1975 prices. (£m)

Monthly Digest for:	All Industries			Manufacturing		
	1979	1980	1981	1979	1980	1981
			£m			
Jan. 1981	+1,610			+166		
July 1981	+1,578	-1,921		+166	-1,396	
Jan 1982	+1,504	-2,128		+211	-1,252	
July 1982	+1,404	-2,108	-1,932	+194	-1,192	-1,014
Jan. 1983	+1,782	-1,555	-1,871	+194	-1,192	-1,014
July 1983	+1,792	-1,538	-1,824	+194	-1,192	-1,014

4 The determinants of stockbuilding

The reasons for holding stocks can be divided into three categories: stocks held to enable a firm to conduct transactions and stocks held for precautionary and speculative motives. [2] The predominant reason for holding stocks, to conduct transactions, occurs because firms are unable to synchronise the receipt and the use in manufacturing or sale of goods for technological reasons. Manufacture and distribution take time and so firms have to hold stocks in the form of work in progress and finished goods. Also there are various indivisibilities and economies of scale associated with the production, transportation and storage of large batches of goods and transactions which increase the stocks firms have to hold if they are to operate efficiently.

There are secondary reasons for holding stocks. Manufacturers and retailers hold stocks to deal with fluctuations in demand which are foreseen; stocks make it possible to smooth production in spite of demand variations, where an even flow of production and of goods to be handled reduces unit costs. In addition, manufacturers and retailers hold stocks as a precaution to deal with unforeseen fluctuations in demand such as occur for most businesses. This precautionary holding of stocks again makes it possible to cushion or smooth production against demand variations. Stocks may be held as a precaution against disruption to supplies or production. These stocks reduce the risk of loss of profit and future business due to an inability to meet demand with prompt delivery.

Speculative stockholding arises from the expectation of future changes in prices and costs. An example of this is provided by users of materials buying extra supplies ahead of expected price rises, although this begs the question why prices are expected to rise if they have not already done so. A possible explanation is that some firms have access to more, or better, information about the forces affecting prices in the markets in which they operate than other agents - the basis of this advantage could be economies of scale in collecting and analysing information. In a competitive situation a firm may not make extra profits by successful speculative stockholding. If all the firms in a trade buy extra supplies ahead of a price rise, they may pass the benefit to buyers; they may be forced by competition to keep their prices down. Alternatively if one firm successfully buys ahead of a price rise, it may keep its product prices down to win increased market share from competitors who have not bought ahead of the price rise. (In many trades it is possible to buy forward, to contract for future delivery; in these trades firms expecting prices to rise, do not have to take delivery and increase their stocks to take advantage of existing prices.)

THE ACCELERATION PRINCIPLE

The three reasons, and particularly the principal transactions explanation for holding stocks, all imply that the volume of stocks will be positively related to the level of sales. The acceleration principle is a formalisation of this insight; it states that the desired level of stocks is proportional to the expected level of sales in the next period. For some accelerator models of stockbuilding actual sales for the most recent period are used as an indicator of sales in the next period.

The accelerator introduces the concept that firms formulate a stock to sales ratio, but there are a number of problems associated with it. No explicit mention of the costs of holding stocks, lags, the general financial and economic climate or of the effects when expectations are not fulfilled are incorporated into it. In seeking an accurate explanation of movements in stockholding then, we must move beyond the simple acceleration principle.

A development of the simple accelerator is the flexible accelerator which allows for lags. It is assumed that firms do not adjust their actual stocks to the desired level in one period and that stockbuilding is a function of expected sales and the actual level of stocks held. There are lags between the placing of orders and the receipt of goods because production and distribution takes time, and there are costs of changing rates of production. Lags also occur because firms may suffer from inertia; there may be delays between evidence of changes in market conditions and managers responding to those changes.

So far it has been assumed that actual sales and production match expected sales and production. In practice they rarely do, so unplanned changes in stocks occur. (Unplanned changes in stocks may be greater in industries in which some or all firms change their output, rather than prices, in response to changes in demand.) Now planned investment in stocks will be affected by past deviations of sales and output from planned levels. Actual investment in stocks will equal intended investment and unexpected sales whether these are positive or negative.

THE COSTS OF HOLDING STOCKS

The stocks to sales ratio would be expected to move inversely with the cost of holding stocks. Firms which borrow money to finance the stocks they hold will tend to reduce their stocks to sales ratio as interest rates rise. Interest rates represent the opportunity cost of finance, so firms which use their equity capital and do not borrow to finance stocks may also reduce their stocks to sales ratio when interest rates rise. There are other costs of holding stocks such as the cost of storage space, the deterioration of products and maintenance and handling costs.

The expected costs of holding stocks are complicated by a number of factors. Decisions about stocks interact with decisions about the costs of production, employment and redundancy. One way for a manufacturer to reduce stocks of finished goods is to make shorter production runs or smaller batches more often, but this increases unit production costs. Destocking may necessitate lay offs or even redundancy for employees, and managers try to avoid these because of the costs of redundancy, retraining, and for social reasons. (In trades where goods are made to order the scope for controlling rates of production by changing stocks of finished goods is more limited.)

In practice the net costs of holding stocks are affected by the treatment of changes in stocks held for computing taxable profits. The changes in the rules for stock relief and their implications for the costs of stockbuilding are described in

Chapter 5. In brief the rules encouraged many firms to increase stocks between 1975 and 1980.

THE OPTIMUM LEVELS OF STOCKS

Ideally firms would calculate an optimum combination of prices (where they have some freedom to set prices) rates of production and rates of investment in stocks for each period, depending upon their initial stocks, their expected sales, the expected rates of inflation for inputs and expected interest rates. In practice many firms do not attempt detailed calculation of the optimum rate of production or level of stocks to hold. Levels of stocks are determined by decisions based on the judgement of managers, accountants and production engineers. They may intuitively hit on the optimum level of stocks, or something close to it, but slack can exist, and stocks exceed the optimum level. The point that levels of stocks and stockbuilding are not necessarily tied to economic variables closely is important.

We now have a framework within which to discuss changes in stocks. The factors determining these are expected changes in sales, the stocks to sales ratio, expected interest and inflation rates and any slack in existing levels of stocks. By considering each of these factors, possible explanations for the destocking which occurred in 1980 and 1981 can be developed.

A REDUCTION IN SALES

A reduction in expected sales would reduce stockholding through a constant stocks to sales ratio. A reduction in expected sales would also have an effect on that ratio, depending on the expected duration of the fall in sales. We start with reasons for a rise in the ratio. In the short run there may be involuntary accumulation of stocks if sales are lower than expected. Firms will not necessarily consider this to be a particularly bad thing, for one aim of stockholding is to smooth production levels when sales fluctuate. Similarly firms may produce for stock to make use of employees as an alternative to lay offs.

A contraction in the level of demand may not produce an equal percentage reduction in stocks owing to indivisibilities in the latter. Moreover some firms may take deliberate action to increase stocks, especially of finished goods, in order to be able to offer quick delivery and so reduce the fall in sales.

In addition new lines may be introduced to diversify from those areas in which sales are falling. This may lead to a build up of work in progress and finished goods before sales increase. Also suppliers may speed up deliveries at a time of slack demand.

Firms may take different counteraction to reduce their stocks to sales ratios. They may simply take greater risks of running short of some stocks. If there is a general recession, firms can rely on getting new supplies quickly. Firms may concentrate their production at fewer factories to cut costs of all sorts, especially where a fall in sales is expected to be permanent. Concentrating successive stages of production at a single site reduces stock levels by eliminating some stocks in transit, and horizontal rationalisation of production at fewer factories may cut duplication of precautionary stocks. Companies may stop making unprofitable lines and eliminate stocks of those lines, and this could reduce the stocks to sales ratio. A fall in demand causes firms to search for improved efficiency including methods of reducing their stocks to sales ratios.

INTEREST RATES AND PRICES

Although the transactions motive provides the main explanation for the holding of stocks, other causes of changes in stocks could be far more important than changes in demand.

If the expected rate of appreciation of stocks falls, or the expected rate of interest rises, this will reduce stocks; an increase in real interest rates encourages firms to 'economise' on stocks by making some stockholding unprofitable. High interest rates serve as a deterrent to methods of trying to raise sales by deliberately building up stocks or entering new lines of production. Also high money and/or real interest rates could shock managers into reviewing the levels of stocks held.

A credit squeeze imposed in order to control the money supply could prevent companies borrowing money, even if they were willing to pay higher interest rates. High interest rates combined with lower demand place firms under considerable pressure. Their ability to borrow is restricted because their after-interest profits, cash flow and the value of their assets, including goodwill, are reduced. In such circumstances firms may reduce employment and/or sell or lease factory space in order to ease the pressure. Stock reductions are important in these circumstances because firms can alter stocks quickly to improve their cash flow. The extent of any slack in stock levels will affect the extent of destocking caused by a shock or a financial squeeze.

Wicksell suggested that stocks rose during recessions and fell during recoveries. He obtained some evidence from Swedish companies that this relationship applied. Apart from the reasons given here for increasing stocks during recessions, Wicksell referred to low interest rates as a factor. [3] In a general equilibrium type model of a decentralised market economy, a recession caused by a shock would be expected to lead to falling prices and interest rates. Low interest rates would pull forward expenditure from the future, including expenditure on stockbuilding. In fact inflation was rapid and real interest rates rose during the 1980/81 recession.

CHANGES IN EXPECTATIONS

Expectations could be an exceedingly important factor in the determination of changes in stock levels. The latest development in this area is the concept of 'rational expectations' which asserts that agents will make the best possible use of all the available information in forming their expectations.

One might expect such a theory to predict fairly stable stock levels, since a single new piece of information would not normally cause large changes in expectations if all previous information is already utilised fully. Certainly, many proponents of rational expectations have seen them as an essentially stabilising phenomenon. However, major events, or shocks, such as a substantial rise in the price of oil or the election of a Government with a different economic philosophy, could lead to a widespread and substantial changes in expectations. If expectations are not fully formed, so that agents are still collecting data with which to form their expectations, then new information might have very considerable effects upon agents' views of the most likely state of the economy and hence upon stockbuilding. Similarly, if agents attribute very similar probabilities to the likelihood of several different levels of sales, then an additional piece of information could cause considerable changes in rational expectations.

The theory of rational expectations has been criticised on the grounds that, however logically sound, it does not represent the way businessmen in the real world behave. Keynes wrote in the General Theory of the possibility of changes in 'animal spirits' causing large changes in firms' investment behaviour. [4] If businessmen are subject to such changes in expectations at an aggregate level and for no readily discernable reason, or their reactions to events are exaggerated, even irrational, then one would predict that large changes in stock levels would occur from time to time as a result of changes in expectations.

The underlying point is that, however businessmen form their expectations, the outcome of the process could affect stockbuilding. Moreover, whether expectations are formed rationally or irrationally (in the 'animal spirits' sense) they could be subject to considerable fluctuation.

DESTOCKING AS A SOURCE OF RECESSION

The importance of destocking in the 1980/81 recession was examined in Chapter 3. The accelerator approach to explaining changes in stocks implies that they are caused by changes in other components of demand; destocking would not be a primary cause of recession, though it could amplify a slowdown in the growth of other elements of demand, or changes in the growth of output caused by supply constraints, via a constant stocks to output ratio. However, if the other components of demand were expected to rise and in the event did not do so, this could result in destocking without there being an actual fall in other elements of demand. Stocks would be increased in line with the expected increase in sales. When sales did not rise as expected there would be involuntary stockbuilding and then destocking. Alternatively if interest rates rise and/or there is a credit squeeze, this could lead to a reduction in target stocks to sales ratios and destocking. Once destocking by distributors and or manufacturers is under way, manufacturers' actual sales will fall, and if they cannot distinguish between destocking by their customers and a fall in sales to final buyers, they may reduce their stocks in proportion to the decline in their actual sales. Thus in theory destocking could be a primary source of recession.

THE PRESSURES ON FIRMS TO DESTOCK IN 1980/81

Finally in this chapter the many pressures on firms to destock and the inter-relationships between the pressures are summarised in Diagram 4.1. The external pressures on firms to destock, namely reduced demand, high interest rates, the fiscal contraction (operating through cuts in the cyclically adjusted PSBR), slower inflation and changed rules for stock relief, are underlined. High interest rates and reduced demand directly cause destocking, they also reduce profits and cash flow and

Diagram 4.1

The Pressures on Companies to Destock in 1980/1981

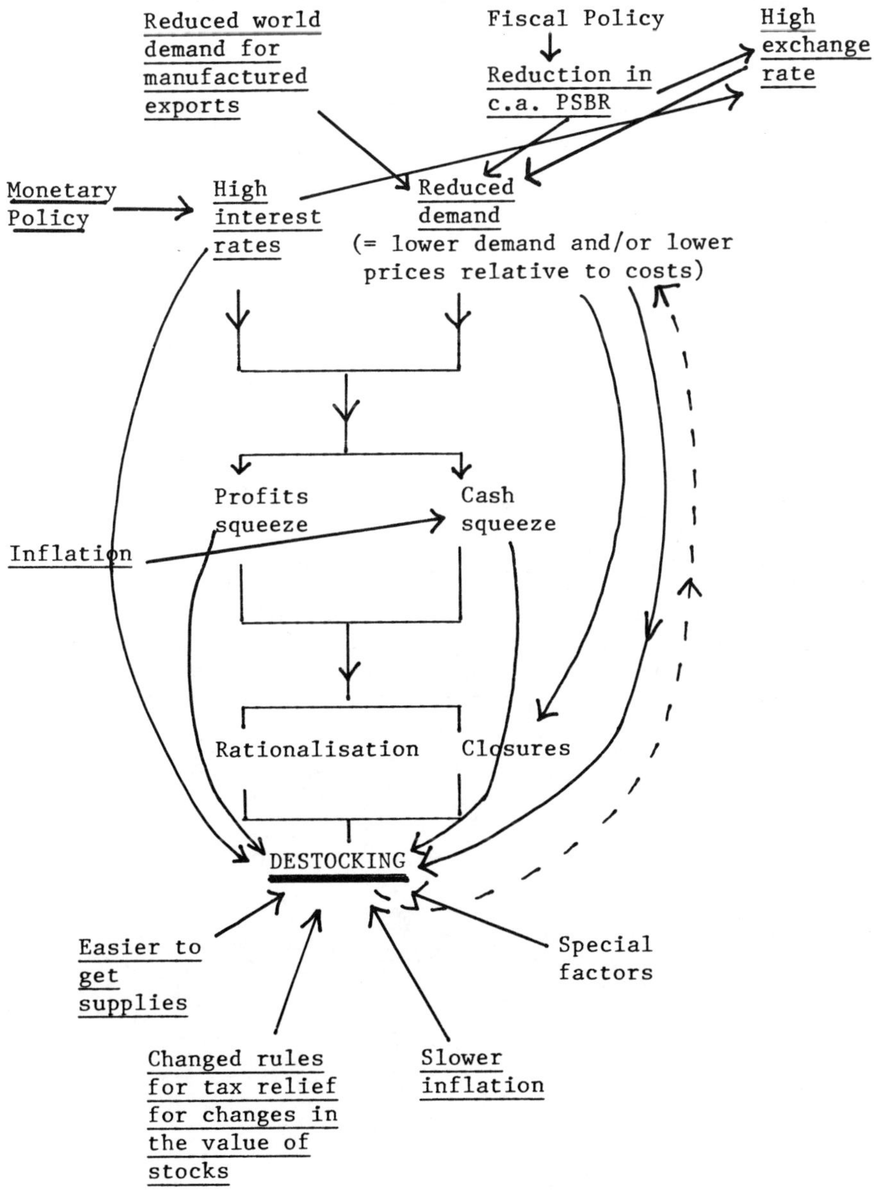

lead to a profits and cash flow squeeze. Although inflation slowed between 1979 and 1982, the continuing inflation increased the cash squeeze; firms had to finance stocks at higher prices. Firms' reactions to these pressures included closing factories and rationalising production which could make possible a reduction in stocks. In turn destocking causes a reduction in demand for the products of other firms; this is indicated in the diagram by the loop from destocking to reduced demand.

NOTES

[1] Sources which were particularly useful in the preparation of this survey included 'Inventories and Business Cycles' by Moses Abramovitz, New York, 1950; 'The Trade Cycle' by R.C.O. Mathews, Cambridge, 1959; 'Planning Production, Inventories and Work Force' by C.C. Holt, F. Modigliani, J.F. Muth and H.A. Simon, Englewood Cliffs, 1960 and 'Determinants of Business Investment' by R. Eisner and R.H. Strotz, Englewood Cliffs, 1963.

[2] These categories are analogous to those used by Keynes for analysing the demand for holding money.

[3] Knut Wicksell, 'Interest and Prices'.

[4] 'Thus if the animal spirits are dimmed and the spontaneous optimism falters, leaving us to depend on nothing but mathematical expectation, enterprise will fade and die; - though fears of loss may have a basis no more reasonable than hopes of profit had before'. General Theory, p. 162.

5 Tax relief for changes in stocks

MERRETT AND SYKES

Tax relief for changes in stocks was introduced in 1974, a year of political, economic and financial turmoil. By the end of September, 1974, the FT-Actuaries 'All Share Index' had halved compared to its level at the beginning of January. On 30th September, Professor A.J. Merrett and Mr Allen Sykes published an influential article describing the decline in real profitability of British industry. [1] Their article included the estimates of profits shown in Table 5.1.

The important point Merrett and Sykes were making was that the 29 per cent rise in gross profits between 1972 and 1973 was a misleading guide to the profitability of industry. They argued that the stock appreciation included in profits was 'wholly fictitious profits' and that after deducting depreciation, stock appreciation, interest and taxes from gross profits, net profits had fallen by 43 per cent in money terms between 1972 and 1973. Moreover there was 'reason to believe (the) position (was) further deteriorating in 1974.'

Merrett and Sykes argued 'that companies are taxed on their stock appreciation as if it was a genuine betterment of a company's position', but in their view stock appreciation was fictitious profit, and should be excluded from taxable profits. The implied principle is that companies (and other taxpayers) should pay taxes on real income - income which represents an

Table 5.1
Estimates of Profits made by Merrett and Sykes

	1972	1973	Percentage change between 1972 and 1973
	£m		
Gross Profits	7,981	10,284	29
Less Replacement Depreciation	2,353	2,732	16
Less Stock Appreciation	1,105	2,516	128
Pre Tax Profits	4,523	5,036	11
Less Interest and Preference Dividends	1,483	2,372	60
Net Profit	3,040	2,664	-12
Tax	1,600	1,839	15
Net of Tax Profits	1,440	825	-43

increase in real wealth, and not be taxed on income needed to maintain wealth in real terms. For a company which finances its stocks from its equity capital, profits equivalent to an increase in the value of stocks in line with the general rate of inflation are not real profits, these profits are required to maintain that part of the company's equity capital invested in stocks, in real terms. Put another way, a firm which finances all of its stocks from its equity capital and holds a constant volume of stocks through the year, should be allowed to make a deduction from its profits assessable to corporation tax. This deduction should be calculated as a percentage of the replacement value of its stocks at the beginning of the year - the percentage to be the rate of price inflation during the accounting year. The inflation rate would be the rate of inflation operating in the economy which could be measured by the deflator for total final expenditure, a wider measure than the retail price index.

In principle, companies should be permitted to make similar adjustments for inflation in respect of their working capital apart from stocks, debtors and cash balances, financed with equity capital, and other taxpayers besides companies, should be entitled to make equivalent inflation adjustments. For example, taxpayers should be allowed to deduct from interest income received in respect of loans outstanding throughout the year, a percentage of the inflation adjusted amount of the loans at the beginning of the year. The percentage would be the percentage increase in prices between the beginning and end of the year, so that only that part of interest income which is real income would be taxed. However, there is a distinction between the taxation of profits and other income. If the taxation of profits is excessive this may lead to lower investment and hence employment; excessive taxation of other incomes may not have these effects.

GODLEY AND WOOD

In fact the waters were far muddier. Wynne Godley and Adrian Wood challenged Merrett and Sykes's version of the 'Doomsday Machine'. [2] They argued that firms financed their stocks not out of equity capital but by borrowing, and that the inclusion of stock appreciation in profits provided 'a good measure of true profits and a proper basis for taxation'.

Godley and Wood illustrated their argument with the example set out in Table 5.2. It is based upon the following definitions and assumptions:

'(i) The corporate sector is treated as though it were one firm.

(ii) Stocks are valued at cost and profits are defined according to the standard FIFO convention as sales less purchases plus the change in the values of stocks.

(iii) Labour productivity, total real output and the volume of stocks are all constant (which implies that the whole of any change in the value of stocks is stock appreciation). It is assumed that stocks are 100% financed by bank overdrafts.

(iv) 'Periods' are defined as (constant) production periods - the time between the beginning of the manufacture (of an object) and its final sale. Goods manufactured in one period are all sold in the subsequent period; this implies (in combination with (ii)) that the value of stocks at the end of each period is equal to purchases of raw materials and labour in that period.

(v) Prices are determined on the basis of a mark-up of 30% on historical costs; i,e, sales in each period are equal to 1.3 times purchases in the previous period.

(vi) Corporation tax is levied at 33% of profit (conventionally defined as in assumption (ii)).

(vii) In order to isolate the problem of profits and stock appreciation, the whole (very real) problem of the depreciation of fixed capital is sidestepped by assuming that there is no fixed capital (and hence no fixed investment).

(viii) It is also assumed initially that the rate of interest on bank borrowing is zero.

Table 5.2
Stock Appreciation on Stocks Financed by Borrowing

		Periods 1.	2. £	3.
(a)	Purchases by companies	100	130	130
(b)	Sales by companies	130	130	169
(c)	Changes in value of stocks and work progress (= change in (a) between one period and the next) = stock appreciation = change in bank overdraft	0	+30	0
(d)	Level of stocks & work in progress (at cost) end period = bank overdraft	100	130	130
(e)	Accounting profit on FIFO basis (=(b)-(a)+(c))	30	30	39
(f)	Company tax = one third of accounting profit	10	10	13
(g)	Dividends (= remainder of accounting profit)	20	20	26

Column 1 shows how things would look period by period if there were no inflation; the company sector earns £30 accounting profit and nobody would dispute that this is a fair representation of what is its 'true' pre-tax income. This is because (i) having paid £10 in corporation tax it has £20 to spend on dividends and (ii) the net worth of the company sector is unchanged.

The second column shows the first production period in a new era of suddenly accelerated inflation. At the beginning of this period (it is assumed) the price of purchases is jacked up by 30%, making current outlays £130 in the period as a whole. The other lines all now follow by assumption or definition. Prices are a constant mark up on historical costs and therefore do not change (until after the end of the period) while the value of sales at £130 equals the value of purchases. The value of stocks and work in progress has gone up by £30 although (by assumption) there is no volume change in stocks, and accounting profits equal £30 once again, all of this being stock appreciation.

But the accounting profit of £30 in this period of inflation is as true as a measure of profit and as proper a basis for taxation notwithstanding that it is all stock appreciation as it was in the previous period when there was no inflation. £10 is paid in tax, £20 is spent on dividends (without prices having changed) just as in the previous period; moreover this has been achieved (as before) without changing the net worth of the company, because the rise in liquid assets (the value of stocks) is exactly matched by the increase in liquid liabilities (the value of bank overdrafts). At the end of the period, exactly as at the end of each non inflationary period, the 'company' could cease trading having made a surplus of £30 (prices being the same as before) and precisely eliminate its bank overdraft by selling off all its stocks at cost.'

Godley and Wood acknowledged that some stocks are financed out of equity capital not borrowing. As noted earlier, there is a case for adjusting the taxable profits of firms which finance their stocks with equity capital. Using Godley and Wood's numerical example, where the profit mark up and rate of inflation in period 2 are both 30 per cent, if the stocks were financed out of equity capital not borrowing, then the payment of £10 of tax and £20 of dividends would reduce the real equity capital of the sector. At the end of period 2, real equity capital would be reduced by 23 per cent (£30 as a percentage of £130). Godley and Wood did point out that adjustment of incomes for inflation was not generally accepted for computing taxable income and argued that it would be 'highly unjust' to allow adjustment for stock appreciation of equity financed stocks 'without a corresponding change being made in the basis of taxation of every sort of income from wealth.'

The position of firms which finance their stocks with equity capital can be illustrated in another way. Godley and Wood assumed that firms pass on interest charges in their mark-ups and illustrated the effects of this in a separate table. Let us assume that firms are able to pass on increases in the notional interest on their own equity capital used to finance stocks by increasing their mark-ups. Unlike firms which borrow, they would be unable to charge the notional interest against profits. To remove the disadvantage of firms which financed stocks out of equity capital (compared to firms which borrowed to finance stocks and charged interest payments against taxable profits) they could have been allowed to deduct the inflation element of notional interest payments for equity capital used to finance stocks from their taxable profits, instead of deducting stock appreciation. This view of tax relief for stock appreciation highlights the anomaly of tax relief for stock appreciation without other adjustments for inflation. If firms were allowed to deduct notional interest for equity capital used to finance stocks from their taxable profits, this interest would not be taxed at all. In contrast the actual interest payments made by companies which financed their stocks by borrowing would be taxable, depending upon the tax status of the agents receiving the interest. It is also important that there were no provisions in the Price Codes in operation in 1973 and 1974 permitting the passing on of increases in notional interest.

Table 5.3 shows the movement of Gross Trading Profits during the mid-1970's. The assumptions made by Godley and Wood lead to the expectation that gross profits should keep pace with

Table 5.3
Profits of Industrial and Commercial Companies

	(1) Gross Trading Profits including stock appreciation		(2) Column (1) less interest and dividends on preference shares		(3) The deflator for total final expenditure
	£m	Index	£m	Index	Index
1970	6,599	100	5,288	100	100
1971	7,454	113	6,079	115	108
1972	8,787	133	7,254	137	116
1973	11,062	168	8,661	164	128
			(a)		
1974	12,770	194	9,388	178	154
1975	13,037	198	9,674	183	191
1976	16,429	249	12,491	236	223

(a) Break in the series which leads to some exaggeration of gross trading profits less interest from 1974. Prior to 1974 dividends were deducted gross, from 1974 they are deducted net of tax.

Source: ETAS 1984.

inflation, though there would be lags between increases in prices of inputs and gross profits. In 1974 and 1975 profits did not keep pace with inflation. There are other possible explanations apart from firms not passing on increases in input prices and interest rates. Profits would be expected to fall during a recession and in 1973 and 1974 many prices were controlled. The Price Commission claimed that the controls it operated, held down prices. If true, this meant a significant reduction in profits from the level they would have been in the absence of controls. [3]

Godley and Wood realised that stock appreciation could cause problems 'because for one reason or another companies are unable or unwilling to borrow enough from banks or similar institutions to finance the whole of any increase in the value of their stocks.' [4] If the problem is seen to be one of financing stocks during a period of inflation, rather than defining taxable profits, the focus of policy will be the increase in prices of goods held in stock rather than the general rate of inflation in the economy. Also the policies adopted to deal with this problem must take account of the fact that the rate at which the prices of goods held in stock increases, varies between firms.

Plainly the debate about stock relief involves questions of principle and facts. In the remainder of this chapter the actual form of stock relief which was adopted, is described. In Chapter 7 the actual financing of stocks is considered.

STOCK RELIEF

The immediate pressure for tax relief was the financial crisis in capital markets. In his Budget Statement on 12th November 1974, the then Chancellor, Mr Denis Healey, said 'The impact of inflation on the company sector risks forcing thousands of firms to restrict their output and lay off workers in the coming winter not through lack of demand for their products ... but simply through lack of working capital ... I am persuaded that industry needs a substantial immediate improvement of its liquidity through the deferment of tax on that part of the profit which corresponds to the abnormal increase in the value of stock and work in progress'. As Anthony Harris commented in the Financial Times the following day 'the Chancellor very carefully refused to say just what principle was involved'. Also the Chancellor's statement referred to 'deferment' of tax not relief from tax. If the problem was liquidity an interest free loan - the deferred tax - could deal with it. Again Harris's comment was perceptive.

The statement about deferred tax liability 'has little enough meaning so far as companies are concerned: for the deferral in effects rolls on from year to year indefinitely'.

Stock relief was not limited to stock appreciation. Firms were allowed to offset the change between the value of their opening and closing stocks (less a deduction) from their profits assessable to corporation tax. [5] The change in stocks was made up of the price and volume changes. The price changes related to the goods stocked by each firm, not to the overall movement of prices in the economy. The deduction was 15 per cent (later 10 per cent) of the profits assessable to corporation tax before deducting stock relief. This was intended as a 'rough and ready' method of allowing for the normal, or average, increase in the volume of stocks, and it tilted relief away from relatively profitable companies to those with a high stocks to profits ratio. Inclusion of volume changes in the formula for calculating the adjustment had advantages if the problem was to ease liquidity, as firms which increased their stocks in volume terms would require extra working capital.

There were provisions that firms could not deduct increases in volumes of stocks in exceptional cases and that stocks should be held through the year, not just at the end of years, but these provisions seem not be have been fully applied.

There were provisions for clawback. If a firm having claimed stock relief later reduced its stocks, its assessable profits were increased by the reduction in the value of its stocks. If the relief was to ease liquidity, then, if a firm ran down its stocks, it no longer required a loan of the deferred tax.

Stock relief was substantial. For tax payable in 1980, the Inland Revenue estimated the revenue cost of stock relief was about £2bn, compared to the expected yield of mainstream corporation tax of £3bn. Of the total relief, 45 per cent went to manufacturing industry and 25 per cent to distributors, including retailers. [6] The relief varied from year to year depending in part on the rate of inflation.

DRAWBACKS TO THE SYSTEM OF STOCK RELIEF

Stock relief was introduced to deal with the liquidity problems of companies. These were attributable to a combination of factors including the increases in working capital required because of inflation. The recession, higher interest rates, the operation of the Price Code and the disarry of financial markets following the collapse of secondary banks and some property companies were other important causes. The relief was aimed to support firms and hence safeguard employment. The form of stock relief provided did ease the liquidity problems of firms whose stocks increased in value and which had taxable profits. But it could be argued that an equivalent reduction or delay in payment of national insurance contributions would have been a more effective way of safeguarding employment.

A drawback of the relief was that it gave firms with profits assessible to corporation tax a massive incentive to increase the volume of their stocks, simply to pile up stocks. At the margin they could at least postpone a tax liability equivalent to 52 per cent of the increase in the value of their stocks. Further, companies were still allowed to charge interest on loans and overdrafts used to finance stocks against taxable profits; the tax system therefore encouraged firms to borrow in order to finance extra stocks especially during the periods of rapid inflation and hence high interest rates which were to follow. In practice there were also problems for companies which had obtained relief and which wished to run down their stocks. Unless they were then making losses assessable to corporation tax, they had to pay out a large proportion of the proceeds of any stock reduction in clawback taxes. As many companies had not provided for this liability in their balance sheets, repayment of relief would have reduced their retained profits, a part of their equity base, besides draining their working capital.

AMENDMENT OF STOCK RELIEF

By 1980, the 1974 system of stock relief needed amendment because of the scope for abuse. In addition there were urgent demands for changes to allow companies grappling with the 1980/81 recession and financial squeeze to destock without clawback.

In his March 1980 Budget, the Chancellor, Sir Geoffrey Howe, announced changes in tax relief for stock appreciation. In the Budget Statement he said, 'A number of businesses in manufacturing, and certain areas of distribution, are concerned about the recovery charges which they will face as a result of reductions in stock levels likely to arise either because of the general pressure on liquidity, or in some cases as a result of the steel strike. I propose, therefore, to allow a substantial part of the stock relief recovery charge consequent on a reduction of stocks to be deferred for one year.' The

Chancellor also committed the government to a further review of stock relief.

From November, 1980 the system was changed to the one suggested at the beginning of the chapter, except that the inflation rate was calculated from a base weighted index representative for all stocks, prepared by the Department of Industry, not the deflator for total final expenditure. There were also provisions for abating relief on stocks financed by borrowing and trade credit. The clawback provisions were abolished under the new system (except where a business ceased or its trading became negligible) so firms could destock without incurring a corporation tax liability. The principle for allowing stock relief was clarified. The principle that firms which financed stocks out of their equity capital were entitled to deduct stock appreciation from taxable profits was accepted, though the adjustment of income for inflation losses was not accepted for all incomes.

For accounting periods straddling 14 November 1980 companies were given the option of which system of relief they preferred. If companies opted for the old system, increases in stocks between 14th November 1980 and the end of a company's year were excluded. (It would be difficult for many companies to estimate their stocks at 14th November 1980). So at the end of 1980 companies liable to corporation tax - companies making profits in excess of capital allowances - had an incentive to have high stock levels on the 14th November 1980 and at their year end to get tax relief on stocks. Once the clawback provisions ceased to apply to companies (from the end of their accounting years) they had an incentive to run down stocks acquired to gain relief in earlier years to reduce interest payments or to earn interest on the funds released.

Under the revised rules companies had some incentive to have high opening stocks if prices were expected to rise as the inflation adjustment was based on these stocks. (Opening stocks are of course the closing stocks at the end of the previous year). But the incentive was much less. There is normally a period of 21 months between the first day of an accounting period and the date when the tax is payable, so by the end of 1982 stock levels may have been at levels based on the commercial requirements of businesses.

THE EFFECTS OF STOCK RELIEF

The economic significance of the impact of stock relief on stockbuilding varies. Where tax provisions led to extra stocks being held throughout the year that was a significant economic effect. Resources were tied up in stocks. When the run down of stocks occurred it resulted in a reduction of aggregate demand. On the other hand, where companies speeded up purchases at the year end to take advantage of stock relief, this affected stocks for only one or two months. At the macroeconomic level the effect would apply throughout the year at ranging intensity according to a weighted average of company year ends (which are concentrated at the end of December, end of January (for retailers) and the end of March).

NOTES

[1] A.J. Merrett and Allen Sykes, 'The real crisis now facing British Industry', Financial Times, 30 September 1974.

[2] Wynne Godley and Adrian Wood, 'Stock Appreciation and the Crisis of British Industry', first published by the DAE, Cambridge, October 1974. The paper and a supplementary paper were published in the CEPG's 'Economic Policy Review, February, 1975'.

[3] In its February 1975 Review the National Institute estimated that the 'Price Code may have reduced the price level by something of the order of two per cent below what it might otherwise have been.' p. 31.

[4] The Times, 12 November, 1974.

[5] Where stocks were less than £2,000 no relief was available.

[6] Op. cit. p. 5.

6 Notes on stockbuilding as a part of macroeconomic analysis

This chapter records movements of the main stock ratios and examines some of the forces causing the ratios to change. The principal official stock ratics are of manufacturers' stocks to manufacturers' output and retailers' stocks to retail sales. Stocks and retail sales are revalued at 1980 prices and manufacturers' output is measured by the index of production of manufacturing industries; the ratios relate volumes of stocks and measures of the volume of output or sales.

STOCK RATIOS

The manufacturers' stocks to output ratio is not identical to the stocks to sales ratio described in Chapter 4. Stocks at the end of a quarter are related to output during the quarter not to expected future sales. Production for stock as well as for sale is included in the denominator, but sales from stock are excluded from it. For the ratio of retail stocks to retail sales, the denominator, retail sales, includes sales from stocks held by retailers. [1]

Diagram 6.1 and 6.2 show the two ratios and the components of the ratios. Comparing the two sets of data, the growth of manufacturing production and the volume of retail sales slowed during the mid 1970's, but manufacturing production slumped in 1980 and 1981 while retail sales in total held steady. Through

Diagram 6.1 Manufacturing Stocks to Manufacturing Output

(4th Q 1979 = 100)

(a) Indices of Stocks at 1980 prices and Production

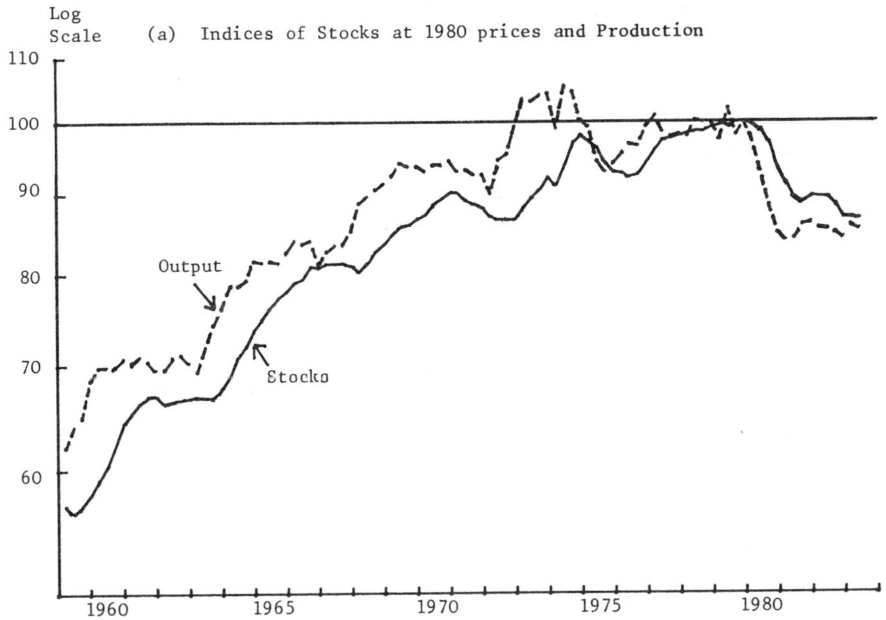

(b) Index of the Stocks to Output Ratio

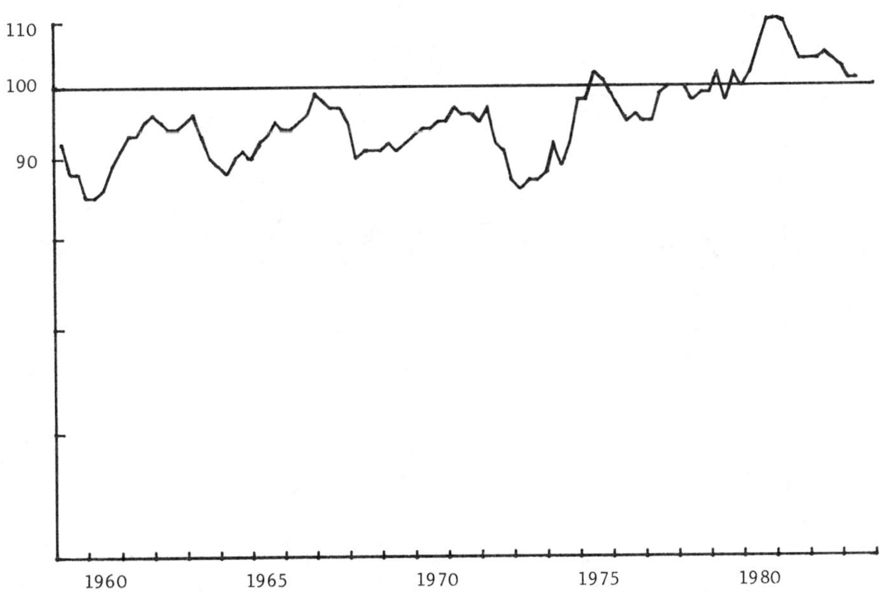

Sources: ETAS and Economic Trends December 1983.

Diagram 6.2 Index of Retail Stocks to Retail Sales

(4th A 1979 = 100)

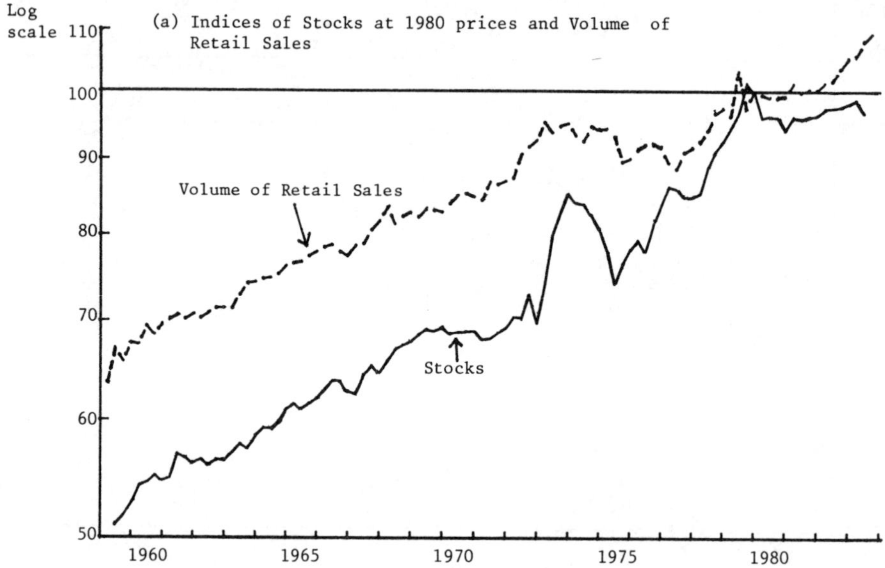

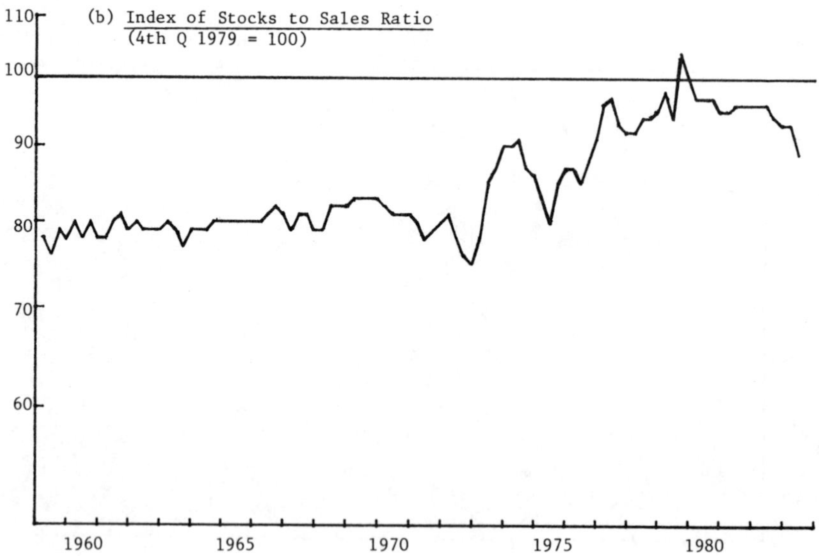

the period since 1959, manufacturing output has had a sharper cyclical pattern than retail sales. Also there is an obvious lag of about a year between changes in manufacturing production and changes in manufacturers' stocks, but any lag between changes in retail sales and retail stocks is less clear. The lag between changes in manufacturers' stocks and production operated in 1979 and 1980; the fall in stocks followed a fall in output but the lag was of about one quarter. This lag indicates that the fall in production led to the fall in stocks not vice versa.

The forces influencing stock changes were described in Chapter 4. One important factor affecting stockbuilding is changes in demand. If, following a change in sales, firms allow their stocks to vary before changing production, then the stocks to output ratio will change before output does. This initial change would be in the opposite direction to the change in sales. When production does respond to sales, the stock ratio may revert to its normal level. The pattern suggested by Diagram 6.1 is that manufacturing industries maintain the level of stocks when production rises and when the growth of production slows stocks increase; the stocks to output ratio moves in the opposite direction to changes in output. After a lag of about a year stocks change in the same direction as the change in output. Until 1973 the ratio of retail stocks to retail sales was relatively stable.

TRENDS

During the 1970's both ratios rose. As a basis for examining events during the 1970's, the stock ratios for the period 1959-71 were used to estimate trend movements, and the results are shown in Diagrams 6.3 and 6.4.

My a priori expectation for the movement of the ratios was for a slow trend decline. This would reflect increased flexibility of manufacturing systems, increased efficiency of stock control systems and economies of scale for stocks attributable to increases in scale of operation, particularly increases in the volume of output of distinct products. Trend changes in the composition of output could affect stock ratios in either direction, depending on the changing balance between trades and product lines with differing stock to output ratios. Finally, increasing imports might be expected to raise the ratios because of longer lead times for ordering and obtaining delivery of fresh supplies. In fact the expectation of trend declines in the ratios is not borne out by the data; both ratios show a cyclical fluctuation around a trend increase of

Diagram 6.3 Index of Ratio of Manufacturers' Stocks to Manufacturing Production (4th Q 1979=100)

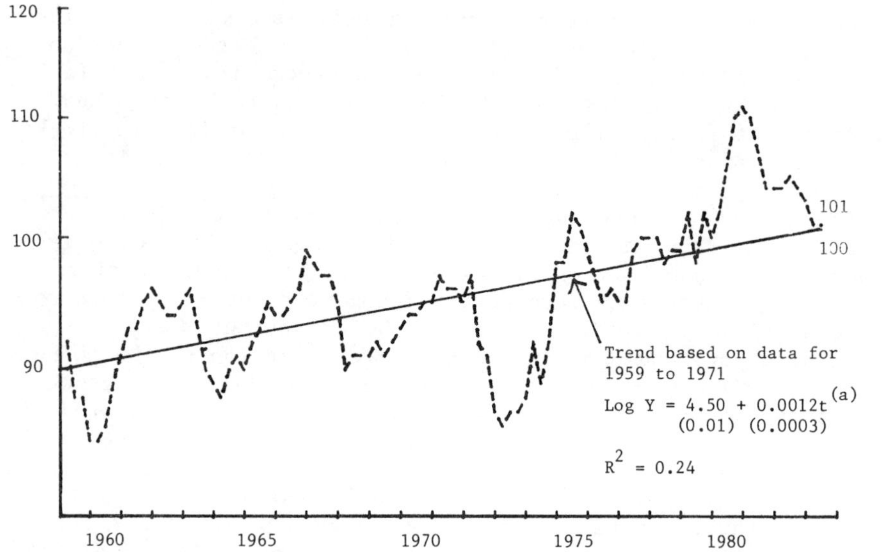

Diagram 6.4 Index of Ratio of Retail Stocks to Retail Sales (4th Q 1979 = 100)

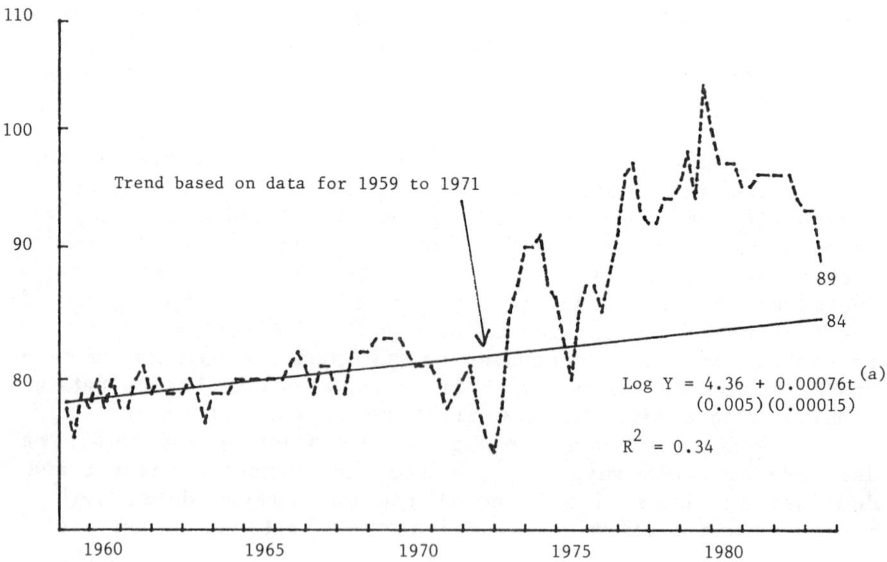

(a) Where t refers to quarters; Q1 1959 = 1; Q2 1959 = 2 ...

less than one per cent a year. [2]

Projected forward beyond 1971, the trends show what would have happened to the stock ratios during the 1970's in the hypothetical event of the forces affecting stockbuilding continuing unchanged. Contrasting actual and the extrapolated trends, the actual ratios moved above the trend levels. For retailers the first break from trend occurred in 1973, while that for manufacturers came later and was less marked. The deviations from trend for the manufacturers' ratio were wide on both sides of the trend during the period to 1975. From 1976 the ratio did not move significantly below the trend. At the end of the second quarter of 1983, manufacturers' stocks were remarkably close to the trend and retailers' stocks were five per cent above their trend level.

Table 6.1 shows the movement of the volume of retail sales and registrations of new cars. There was no growth between 1975 and 1977 followed by rapid growth in 1978 and 1979, with 1980 a year in which sales, apart from food, fell back. Retailers who extrapolated the increases in sales in 1978 and 1979 when placing orders for 1980, built up excess stocks. The Table also shows the burst of sales in the second quarter of 1979 caused by the announcement of an increase in VAT.

CHANGES IN THE STRUCTURE OF MANUFACTURING INDUSTRY

Changes in the pattern of output could have effects on the stocks to output ratio for manufacturing as a whole. The ratio could be affected by the changing balance of output, between industries with high ratios of stocks to output and those with low levels of stocks relative to their output. It is important to evaluate the effects of changes in the pattern of industry on stocks. This was done by taking stocks at the end of 1972 for each industry group, and calculating the effects on stocks for manufacturing industry if the stocks of each industry group increased in line with its production. The resulting index was compared with the index of manufacturing production which indicated the movement of stocks if there was no change in the pattern of production and the stocks to output ratio for each industry group had remained constant. The results are presented in Table 6.2. It can be seen that the two indices diverge very little until 1979, then changes in the pattern of production do increase stocks relative to output. The composition of manufacturing did not alter drastically over the decade, and the changes that took place tended to balance out. For example, the relative importance of chemicals (an industry with a low stocks to output ratio) increased, but output of the

Table 6.1
The Volume of Retail Sales

	Total	Food Retailers	Mixed Retail Businesses	Clothing and Footwear	Household Goods Retailers	Other non Food Retailers	New Registrations of Cars
	Seasonally adjusted			1978=100			
1975	96.6	104.7	90.5	96	88	99	75.4
1976	96.4	102.2	93.4	95	90	97	81.6
1977	94.8	99.7	93.0	89	91	95	86.4
1978	100.0	100.0	100.0	100	100	100	100.0
1979	104.3	104.3	103.9	106	108	100	108.6
1980	104.3	108.8	103.7	105	107	94	94.5
1981	105.5	108.5	106.7	108	110	91	94.7
1982	108.2	109.6	109.6	114	120	89	99.3
1979Q1	101.1	102.9	99.6	101	102	98	100.5
Q2	108.4	104.9	108.2	110	120	104	135.8
Q3	102.5	103.3	102.6	104	104	98	89.8
Q4	105.1	106.1	105.1	108	107	99	108.6
1980Q1	104.5	107.2	104.0	105	107	97	106.6
Q2	104.2	108.5	102.8	104	106	95	92.2
Q3	104.1	107.5	104.1	105	107	93	94.2
Q4	104.2	108.9	103.9	105	107	91	84.9

Source: ETAS 1984

Table 6.2
Effects of Changes in the Pattern of Manufacturing Production on Stocks

	(1) Index of Stocks (with the changing pattern of Production) [a] (1972 = 100)	(2) Index of Manufacturing Production [b] (1972=100)	(1) as a % of (2). Index showing the effects of the changing pattern of production for stock-holding
1972	100	100	100
1973	108.8	109.3	99.5
1974	108.3	108.0	100.3
1975	101.6	100.5	101.1
1976	102.9	102.4	100.5
1977	105.0	104.3	100.7
1978	105.6	105.0	100.6
1979	105.4	104.9	100.5
1980	97.1	95.8	101.4
1981	90.5	89.2	101.5
1982	93.0	88.5	105.1

[a] This index shows what would have happened to stocks if the stocks of each industry group had changed in proportion to changes in its production from 1972.

[b] This index shows what would have happened to stocks if they had changed in line with production and there was no change in the pattern of production.

metals and textile groups fell very steeply and both have lower than average stocks to output ratios. (Information about stocks held by industry groups is summarised in the Appendix to this Chapter.)

The changes in the composition of output in 1980 and 1982 tended to increase the stocks to output ratio for manufacturing industries as a whole; between 1979 and 1982, the effect was an increase of 4.6 percentage points. Diagram 6.3 shows that the stocks to output ratio for manufacturing at the end of 1982 was close to the trend based on data for 1959 to 1971. The calculations made here indicate that stocks may have been below trend at the end of 1982, changes in the composition of output were increasing the ratio [3]

This test examined the effects of changes in the composition of manufacturing production at an industry group level. Changes within industry groups could also affect the stocks to output ratio for manufacturing. The changing composition of retail sales, for example, towards a higher proportion of durables, could affect the ratio of retailers' stocks to sales, but this was not tested.

CATEGORIES OF MANUFACTURERS' STOCKS

The behaviour of the sub-categories of manufacturers' stocks are also of interest. Changes in stocks by categories are shown in Table 6.3. Destocking was concentrated on stocks of raw materials and fuel. Between the end of 1978 and the end of 1982, these fell by 20.8 per cent. The fall in finished goods stocks was relatively mild and was concentrated in the year from the end of the second quarter of 1980.

Stock ratios for the three categories of stocks are shown in Diagrams 6.5 to 6.7. Trends based on data for the years 1959 to 1971 are again shown in the diagrams. For stocks of materials and fuel there is a clear downward trend. For both work in progress and finished goods the trends are for increasing ratios.

The explanations for the diverse trends could be increasing efficiency in stockholding, offset for finished goods by intensified competition which forced manufacturers to hold larger stocks of work in progress and finished products to improve their service to customers. Also there may have been a trend for manufacturers to use imported components which would cut their raw material stocks, and to distribute imports which would increase their stocks of finished goods, relative to their production.

Earlier it was shown that the stocks to output ratio for manufacturing was above trend from the mid-1970's. This departure from trend was concentrated on raw materials and fuel.

Table 6.3

Changes in Manufacturers' Stocks by Categories of Stocks

(at 1980 prices seasonally adjusted)

	Total	Total (4 quarters)	Raw Materials and Fuel	Raw Materials and Fuel (4 quarters)	Work in Progress	Work in Progress (4 quarters)	Finished Goods	Finished Goods (4 quarters)
			£m					
Value of Stocks end December 1978	36,164		12,755		13,138		10,271	
1979 Q1	45		-45		-68		158	
Q2	15		135		1		-121	
Q3	183		32		0		151	
Q4	32	-200	-107	-525	-194	-435	333	760
1980 Q1	-167		-270		-7		109	
Q2	-248		-180		-234		167	
Q3	-636		-387		-192		-56	
Q4	-1,270	-3,421	-414	-1,499	-281	-735	-576	-1,187
1981 Q1	-762		-342		-135		-285	
Q2	-753		-356		-127		-270	
Q3	-162		-167		91		-87	
Q4	219	25	-57	-261	126	189	151	97
1982 Q1	-36		-55		-67		86	
Q2	4		18		39		-53	
Q3	-342		-119		-101		-122	
Q4	-634		-336		-164		-134	
Percentage change Q4 1978 to Q4 1982	-13.2		-20.8		-10.0		-5.3	

Source: ETAS, 1984.

Diagram 6.5

Index of Ratio of Manufacturers' Stocks of Materials and Fuel to Manufacturing Production (4th Q 1979 = 100)

(a) Indices of Stocks and Manufacturing Production

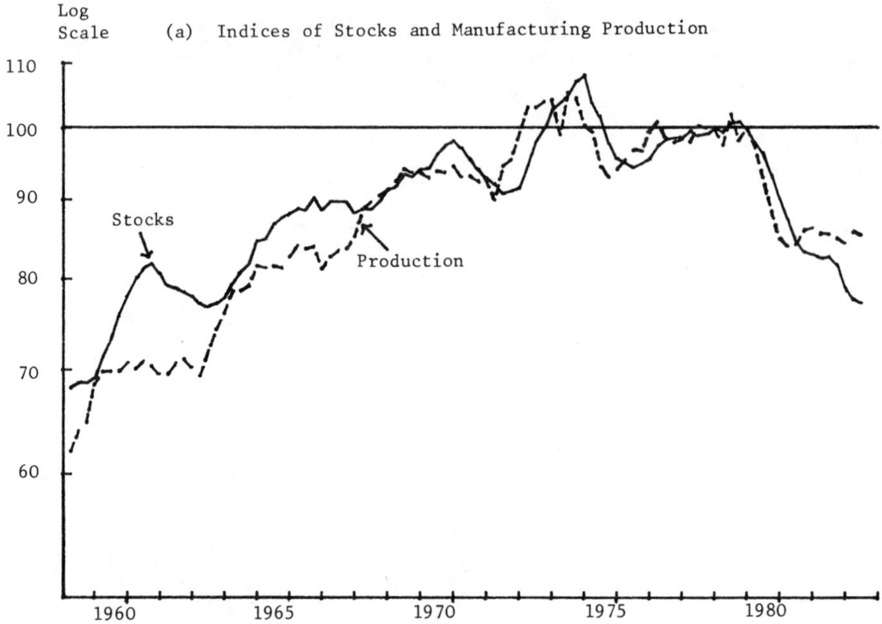

(b) Index of the Ratio of Stocks to Production

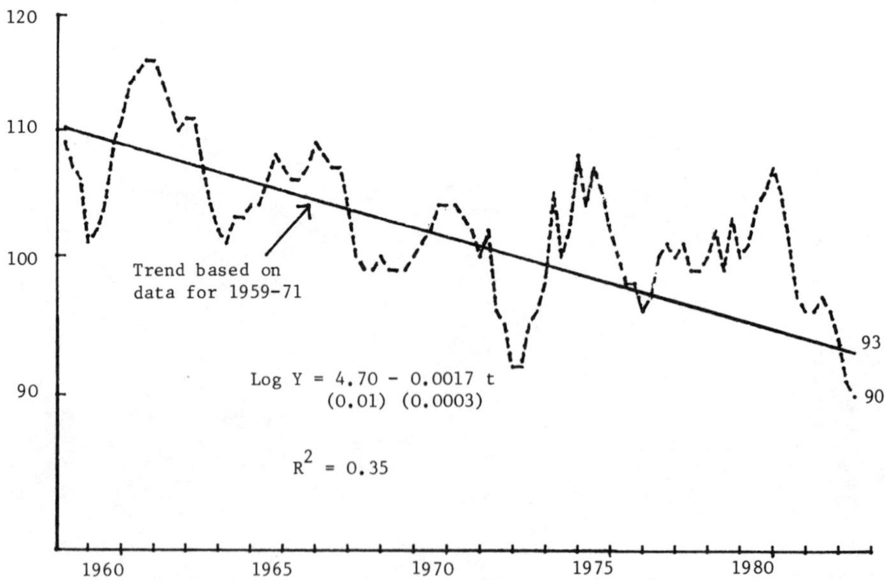

Diagram 6.6 Index of the Ratio of Manufacturers' Work in Progress to Manufacturing Production

(4th Q 1979=100)

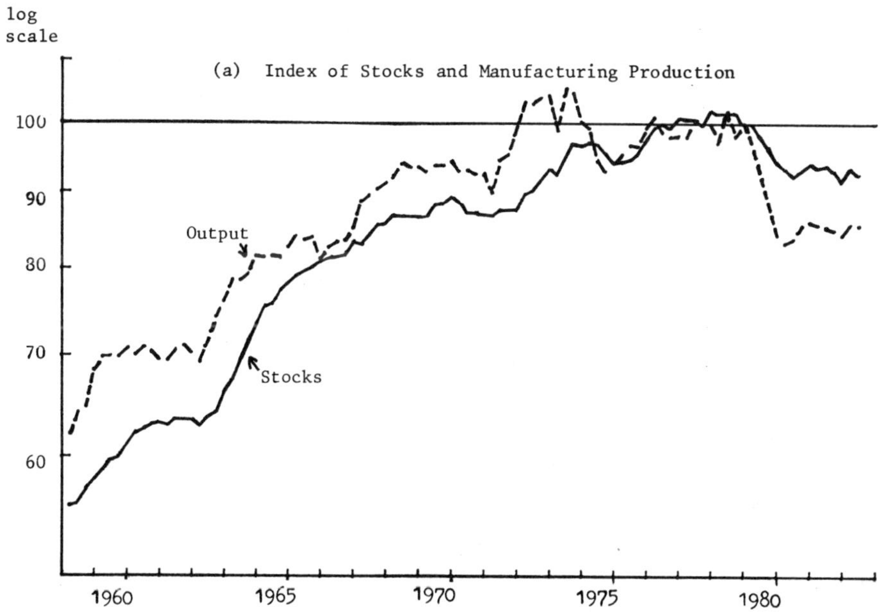

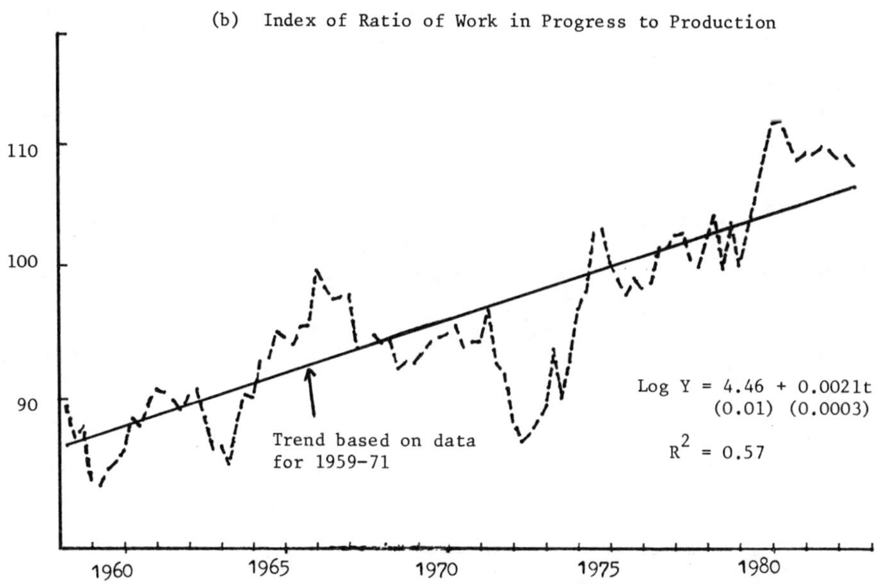

Diagram 6.7 Index of Ratio of Manufacturers' Stocks of Finished Goods to Manufacturing Production (4th Q 1979=100)

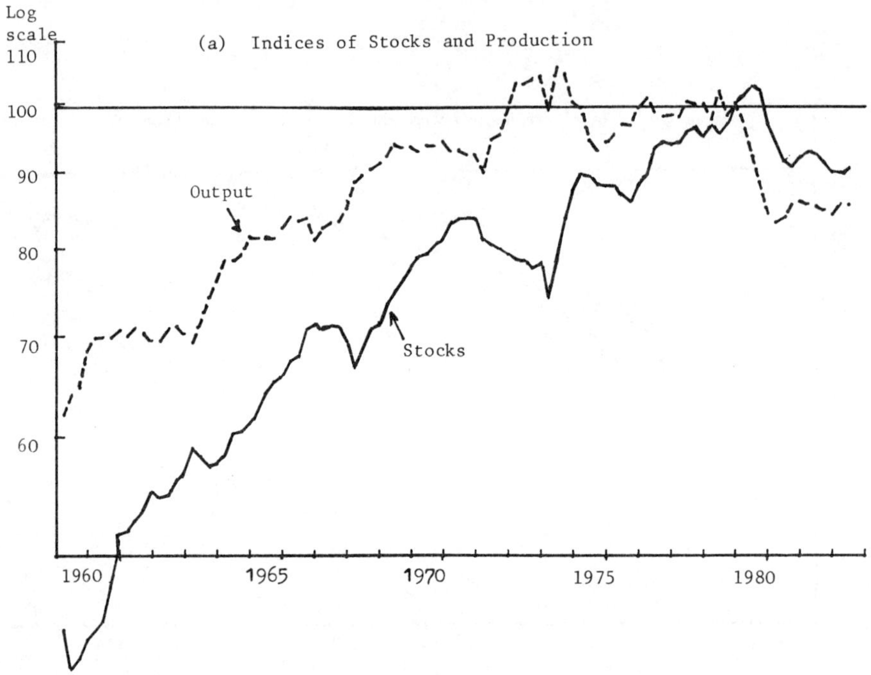

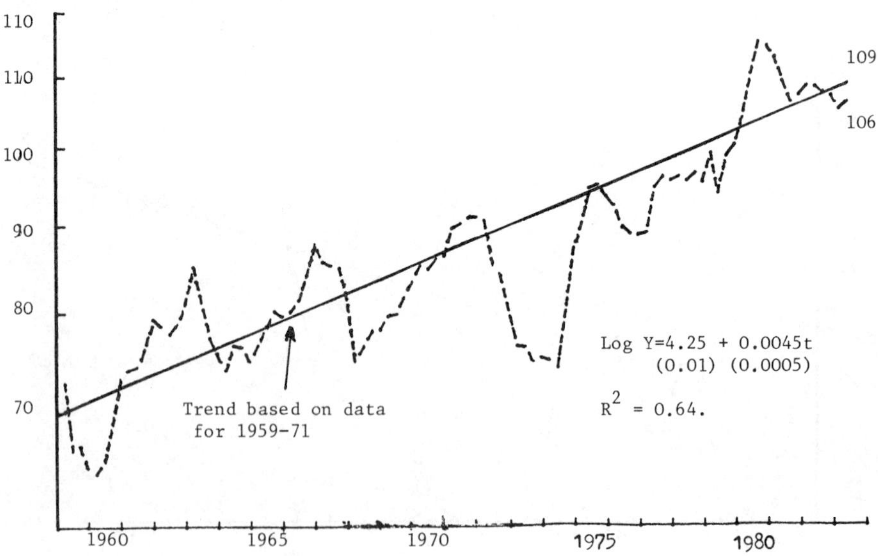

MOVEMENTS OF THE STOCK RATIOS DURING THE PERIOD OF DESTOCKING

Table 6.4 records the recent movements of the stock ratios. The ratios for manufacturers' finished goods and retail stocks increased during 1979. In 1980 the ratios for manufacturers' stocks to output rose as production fell faster than stocks. Between the end of 1979 and the end of 1980 the ratio of manufacturers' finished goods stocks to output rose by 15 percentage points. In contrast the ratio of retail stocks to retail sales fell during 1980, retailers reduced stocks while the volume of sales was steady. During 1981 the ratio of manufacturers' stocks to production fell.

THE SPECULATIVE DEMAND FOR STOCKS

The speculative motive for holding stocks was distinguished in Chapter 4. Stock levels will be influenced by changes in the expected appreciation in value of stocks relative to the expected rate of interest. The speculative motive is not the main motive for holding stocks, but it could be an important factor determining changes in stocks, and even more important for changes in stockbuilding.

To evaluate the scope for firms to gain an advantage by holding stocks some test calculations were made with a rate of interest two percentage points above Treasury Bill rate. [4] This rate of interest and changes in the wholesale price index for materials and fuel are compared in Table 6.5. The comparisons show that it did not pay to borrow to hold stocks of materials and fuel during the period from 1957 to 1971; 1967 was the only year in which the rate of appreciation of stocks exceeded the rate of interest. During 1972 and 1973 appreciation in the value of stocks substantially exceeded the interest cost of holding the stocks. A firm which acquired extra, speculative, stocks of materials and fuel at the beginning of 1972 and held them until the end of the first quarter of 1974 would have had a substantial potential profit. The materials and fuel would have increased in value by 104 per cent and the cumulative interest charge would have been 24 per cent - the net gain would have been 65 per cent on the total cost including interest, less the costs of storage and any deterioration or shrinkage of the materials. Between the first quarter of 1974 and the fourth quarter of 1979, stock appreciation exceeded interest for twelve of the twenty four quarters.

The test calculations play down the incentive provided for stockholding for two general reasons. Firstly some firms do not have to borrow to finance stocks, they use their own

Table 6.4

Movements of the Stock Ratios since the end of 1978 (Seasonally adjusted)

	Manufacturing stocks to Production				Retail Stocks to Retail Sales
	All	Raw Materials and Fuel	Work in Progress	Finished Goods	
	(Ratio for the last quarter of 1978=100)				
1978 Q4	100	100	100	100	100
1979 Q1	103	102	102	104	103
Q2	99	99	98	99	99
Q3	103	103	101	104	109
Q4	101	100	98	105	105
1980 Q1	103	101	101	109	102
Q2	107	104	104	116	102
Q3	111	105	107	121	102
Q4	112	107	110	120	100
1981 Q1	111	105	110	119	100
Q2	108	101	108	115	101
Q3	105	97	107	112	101
Q4	105	96	107	113	101
1982 Q1	105	96	107	114	101
Q2	106	97	108	114	101
Q3	105	96	108	114	99
Q4	104	94	107	113	98

Source: ETAS 1984

Table 6.5

Wholesale Prices of Materials and Fuel and Interest Rates[a]

		(1) Percentage change in wholesale prices	(2) Interest Rates	(3) (1)-(2)[b]	
1957		-10.4	5.3	-15.7	
8		0.9	3.8	-2.9	
9		2.0	5.4	-3.4	
1960		-2.6	4.9	-7.5	
1		0.2	4.4	-4.2	
2		1.0	4.8	-3.8	
3		4.7	5.2	-0.5	
4		0.9	5.6	-4.7	
5		1.4	6.0	-4.6	
6		0.8	6.9	-6.1	
7		8.0	6.3	+1.7	
8		2.0	7.4	-5.4	
9		5.2	8.7	-3.5	
1970		2.5	8.4	-5.9	
1		4.2	6.3	-2.1	
2		14.5	6.1	+8.4	
3		59.3	12.7	+46.6	
4	(1)	11.9	3.6	+8.3	
	(2)	-1.5	3.4	-4.9	+1.9
	(3)	2.1	3.4	-1.3	(+8.8)[b]
	(4)	2.7	3.3	-0.6	
5	(1)	0	3.0	-3.0	
	(2)	3.6	2.9	+0.7	+3.9
	(3)	7.4	3.2	+4.2	(+10.1)[b]
	(4)	5.3	3.3	+2.0	
6	(1)	7.6	2.7	+4.9	
	(2)	7.3	3.2	+4.1	

		(1) Percentage change in wholesale prices	(2) Interest Rates	(3) (1)-(2)	
1976	(3)	6.7	3.4	+3.3	+12.2
	(4)	4.0	4.1	-0.1	(+18.3)[b]
1977	(1)	4.3	3.2	+1.1	
	(2)	-1.0	2.4	-3.4	-11.8
	(3)	-2.6	2.1	-4.7	(-7.0)[b]
	(4)	-2.8	2.0	-4.8	
1978	(1)	2.4	2.0	+0.4	
	(2)	1.9	2.6	-0.7	-4.0
	(3)	-0.8	2.8	-3.6	(-1.3)[b]
	(4)	3.3	3.4	-0.1	
1979	(1)	3.5	3.6	-0.1	
	(2)	7.8	3.6	+4.2	+9.1
	(3)	4.7	4.0	+0.7	(+16.9)[b]
	(4)	8.7	4.4	+4.3	
1980	(1)	5.7	4.7	+1.0	
	(2)	0	4.6	-4.6	-8.8
	(3)	0.2	4.2	-4.0	(-0.1)
	(4)	2.8	4.0	-1.2	
1981	(1)	5.9	3.6	+2.3	
	(2)	5.4	3.5	+1.9	-1.5
	(3)	2.8	4.1	-1.3	
	(4)	-0.1	4.3	-4.4	
1982	(1)	-0.2	3.9	-4.1	
	(2)	2.8	3.8	-1.0	-5.2
	(3)	1.0	3.1	-2.1	
	(4)	4.9	2.9	+2.0	

a Wholesale prices of inputs of basic materials and fuel purchased by manufacturing industry and Treasury Bill rate + 2 per cent p.a.

b The figures in brackets are described in the text

Sources: Monthly Digests of Statistics.

capital. They consider the opportunity cost of the capital tied up in stocks which was perhaps two percentage points lower than the rate of interest used for the exercise, giving these firms more incentive to hold stocks. More important the incentive was increased where firms could charge interest against taxable profits or paid tax on interest received, but paid no tax on stock appreciation - the position for many companies from 1974 until 1980. With a corporation tax rate of 52 per cent, the interest cost of holding stocks was halved. The effect of halving the interest charge is shown in brackets for the years 1974 to 1980 in Table 6.5. The appreciation of stocks exceeded net interest payments in 1974, 1975, 1976 and 1979. In addition a firm which increased its stocks in volume terms and had profits assessable to corporation tax, could avoid tax equivalent to 52 per cent of the cost of the additional stocks.

There are many qualifications to these test calculations as a guide to the return from holding stocks. It is the expected, not the actual, price changes which are important, and these test calculations are based on changes in actual prices. Nor is any allowance made for the costs of storage space for holding stocks or any physical deterioration in stocks. [5]

The test calculations can be put in a different perspective. There are advantages for holding stocks to meet unexpected orders promptly, in case of disruption to supplies caused by strikes, etc. The cost penalty for holding stocks was much lower during the 1970's than during the 1960's.

Increasing stock ratios for manufacturing and retailing after 1973 were shown earlier in this Chapter. The relationship between inflation and interest rates, and the tax treatment of stocks and interest, could explain this movement. When inflation slowed in 1981 and 1982 and the tax incentives to hold stocks had been removed, the ratios fell. The decline in output in 1980 and 1981 was another factor causing destocking.

MACROECONOMIC MODELS

In this chapter some relationships between stockbuilding and output, inflation and interest rates have been considered. Another approach to analysing stockbuilding is to model the economy and account for destocking in terms of past economic relationships. It was outside the scope of this project to prepare a new model for this purpose, but recent reviews of two leading econometric models of the economy have been published. [6] They report that these models failed to predict the extent of destocking in 1980; destocking was more severe than relationships based on past data predicted. [7]

NOTES

[1] The volume of retail sales (retail sales revalued at 1980 prices) is a measure of the 'output' of the retail sector.

[2] The choice of 1971 as the cut off year is of some significance for estimating the trends. If 1972 had been chosen this would have reduced the estimated trend rates of increase; the ratios for manufacturing and retailing fell between 1971 and 1972. However, 1972 was a year in which the increase in demand was unusually rapid.

[3] The calculations are not conclusive because there could have been trend changes in the composition of output during the base period.

[4] This rate of interest was used as a guide to the rate paid by large, secure borrowers.

[5] The tests are for the whole of manufacturing, some industries experienced greater incentives for stockbuilding. For example the prices of inputs purchased by the chemical industry rose by 50 per cent between January, 1979 and January, 1980, when the price of oil was rising.

[6] Papers presented to the Bank of England's Panel of Academic Consultants, No. 15. '<u>Factors Underlying the Recent Recession</u>'. The paper describes simulations of the National Institute and London Business School models. The National Institute's model and its operation are described in '<u>Employment Output and Inflation</u>' edited by A. Britton, London, 1983. This book lists many econometric studies of stockbuilding on pages 38 and 39.

[7] There are inherent problems for this type of analysis because the 1979-80 recession was deeper than earlier postwar recessions, and the government adopted different economic policies, it raised interest rates, in earlier recessions governments reduced interest rates.

Appendix Stocks held by industry groups

In this Appendix data for six broadly defined groups of manufacturing industries are examined, and stocks of materials and fuel, work in progress and finished goods are distinguished. These statistics are not very reliable. Disentangling volume and price changes poses particular problems when inflation is as rapid as during the 1970's. The data show that different industry groups have different stock structures and that the stock ratios for industry groups do not move together closely.

Table 6.A.1 on pages 70 and 71 shows stocks in 1978 and changes in the volume of stocks since 1978 for industry groups. The engineering industry group accounted for almost a half of all stocks in 1978, and a half of the engineering sector's stocks were work in progress. The reduction in material and fuel stocks and work in progress since 1978 applies to all the industry groups. Work in progress and finished goods stocks held by the engineering group fell relatively little; nevertheless destocking by the engineering group accounted for 45 per cent of destocking by manufacturing industries. The next most important industry group for destocking was 'other manufacturing' with 18 per cent of the total.

Percentage changes in stocks, output and the stocks to output ratios for the industry groups are also shown in Table 6.A.1. If the decline in demand and output caused the destocking, then the industries in which output declined most would be expected to show the largest reductions in stocks. If the financial squeeze and particularly high interest rates were the principal factor, then the destocking would be spread more evenly. In fact the data do not provide a conclusive answer. There is a positive but not close link between changes in output and destocking. For example, the output of the food industry group increased and the industry destocked less than any other group apart from chemicals, but it did reduce its stocks substantially.

For all the industry groups apart from food, the stocks to output ratio increased between the end of 1978 and the end of 1982. Output fell more than stocks; prima facie evidence that stocks fell in response to a decline in demand. If stocks had fallen more than output as they did for the food group, this would suggest that other forces as well as the fall in demand were causing destocking.

Table 6.A.2 on page 72 shows the value of end of year stocks in relation to value added, by type of stock for the industry groups. A comparison is made between the position at the end of 1972, 1978 and 1981. The ratios of stocks to value added are in current price terms and are affected by changes in the prices of materials and fuel relative to other costs of production, as well as changes in the volume of stocks relative to output. Between the first quarter of 1972 and the last quarter of 1980, prices of materials and fuel purchased by manufacturing industry increased twenty four per cent more than home costs. This differential would increase the value of stocks, particularly stocks of materials and fuel relative to value added. Differential movements of prices within years also affect the percentages.

Starting with the data for 1972, a notable feature for the food industry group is the high ratio of materials and fuel to net output. This may reflect a high proportion of imports and the fact that harvested goods must to stored as soon as they become available. The group of industries collected in the chemicals group has a very low ratio of work in progress. This may be due to the continuous-flow nature of production in some of these industries, ensuring that material is not classified as work in progress for long. The large engineering group is characterised by a high ratio of total stocks to value-added and a particularly high ratio for work in progress reflecting the long time span required to make and assemble complex engineering products.

Table 6.A.1. Changes in Manufacturers' Stocks by Industry Group (£m 1980 prices)

	Value of stocks held at the end of 1978	As percentage of total	Changes in Stocks: 1979	1980	1981	1982	end 1978 to end of 1982	as % of stocks at end of 1978	as % of total de-stocking	Percentage change: in output 1978Q4 to 1982Q4	in the stocks to output ratio end 1978 to end 1982 (a)
Manufacturing:											
Metals											
Materials and fuel	1,310	3.6	59	-157	-80	-65	-243	-18.5	5.4		
Work in progress	422	2.5	81	-82	-60	-37	-98	-10.6	2.2		
Finished products	597	1.7	-10	27	-45	-32	-60	-10.1	1.3		
Total	2,829	7.8	130	-212	-185	-134	-401	-14.2	8.9	-22.6	10.9
Chemicals and man-made fibres											
Materials and fuel	1,415	3.9	55	-135	-106	-19	-205	-14.5	4.5		
Work in progress	654	1.8	-51	-78	34	8	-87	-13.3	1.9		
Finished products	1,577	4.4	239	-148	-62	13	42	2.7	-0.9		
Total	3,646	10.1	243	-361	-134	2	-250	-6.9	5.5	-8.9	2.2
Metal goods, engineering and vehicles											
Materials and fuel	5,008	13.8	-79	-403	-421	-262	-1165	-23.3	25.8		
Work in progress	8,543	23.6	-267	-343	122	-76	-546	-6.4	12.1		
Finished products	3,908	10.8	95	-89	-220	-64	-278	-7.1	6.2		
Total	17,459	48.3	-251	-835	-519	-402	-2007	-11.5	44.5	-15.8	5.1

Table 6.A.1 continued

Food, drink and tobacco											
Materials and fuel	1,996	5.5	-27	-189	-89	-8	-313	-15.7	6.9		
Work in progress	1,521	4.2	-1	-49	-84	-139	-273	-17.9	6.1		
Finished products	1,550	4.3	69	-9	-30	-5	25	1.6	-0.6		
Total	5,067	14.0	41	-247	-203	-152	-561	-11.1	12.4	+0.3	-11.4
Textiles, clothing and footwear											
Materials and fuel	903	2.5	-	-146	-83	-16	-245	-27.1	5.4		
Work in progress	552	1.5	-7	-87	-25	-20	-139	-25.2	3.1		
Finished products	886	2.4	87	-58	-68	-49	-88	-9.9	2.0		
Total	2,341	6.5	80	-291	-176	-85	-472	-20.2	10.5	-27.3	9.8
Other Manufacturing											
Materials and fuel	2,123	5.9	7	-221	-144	-121	-479	-22.6	10.6		
Work in progress	947	2.6	-16	-76	-31	-30	-153	-16.2	3.4		
Finished products	1,752	4.8	41	-79	-65	-86	-189	-10.8	4.2		
Total	4,822	13.3	32	-376	-240	-237	-821	-17.0	18.2	-19.8	3.5
Total Manufacturing											
Materials and fuel	12,755	35.3	15	-1,251	-922	-492	-2,650	-20.8	58.7		
Work in progress	13,138	36.3	-261	-714	-45	-293	-1,313	-10.0	29.1		
Finished products	10,271	28.4	521	-356	-491	-223	-549	-5.3	12.2		
Total	36,164	100.0	275	-2,321	-1,458	-1,008	-4,512	-12.5	100.0	-15.5	3.6

(a) $\left(\frac{100 + \text{col }(8)}{100 + \text{col }(10)} \times 100\right) - 100$

Source: National Income and Expenditure 1983.

Table 6.A.2.

Stocks as a percentage of Output

(value of stocks at the end of the year as a percentage of net output for the year for broad industry groups)

	1972				1978				1981			
	Materials and fuel	Work in progress	Finished goods	Total stocks	Materials and fuel	Work in progress	Finished goods	Total stocks	Materials and fuel	Work in progress	Finished goods	Total stocks
	%	%	%	£m	%	%	%	£m	%	%	%	£m
Metals	15.5	8.1	8.7	595	23.5	16.1	11.4	2,188	21.4	16.0	11.4	2,327
		32.3				51.0				48.8		
Chemicals and man-made fibres	9.7	7.0	12.5	770	14.0	7.8	15.9	2,525	14.5	7.8	19.1	3,239
		29.1				37.7				41.4		
Metal goods, engineering and vehicles	24.3	36.4	18.1	5,178	25.9	44.6	19.2	14,812	22.9	47.5	20.3	18,316
		78.7				89.7				90.7		
Food, drink and tobacco	30.0	21.2	20.1	1,602	30.9	18.4	22.2	3,976	21.4	16.3	21.1	4,824
		71.2				71.5				58.8		
Textiles, clothing and footwear	22.4	13.3	18.0	819	24.3	14.3	22.5	2,054	21.1	13.1	25.0	2,106
		53.7				61.0				59.2		
Other manufacturing	20.9	9.1	23.1	1,615	24.2	10.5	21.8	4,079	21.9	10.0	22.4	5,010
		53.1				56.5				54.2		
Total manufacturing	21.2	20.6	17.4	10,567	24.0	24.8	19.0	29,632	21.0	25.4	20.1	35,819
		59.1				67.9				66.6		

Source: National Income and Expenditure 1983.

Turning to the 1978 data, there is a general increase in the percentages, with the increases for the metals group being pronounced. For the engineering group only the percentage for work in progress rose sharply. The notable contrast between the percentages for 1978 and 1981 is the decline in the percentage of materials and fuel held by the food group.

7 The record of the sample of companies which destocked

THE SAMPLE.

The sample of companies which destocked was not a random sample of all companies. The method of selecting companies to approach for assistance with the study is described in Appendix A. In brief, companies which had sales of more than £20 million in their latest accounting year and which reduced their stocks substantially in that year were included in the sample [1], but there was a bias towards selecting companies whose head offices were in the South East of England. The positive response rate from those companies which were approached and whose activities were concentrated in manufacturing industries was 46 per cent, and from retailers eighty per cent. The positive response rate from the small number of giant manufacturing companies approached was much higher than for manufacturing companies generally. [2] There was some bias towards companies in financial difficulties or severely affected by the recession, not to assist with the study. The implications of this bias are considered in Appendix A. Of the sample of forty two companies which destocked, twenty six operated primarily in manufacturing industries, ten in retailing and six distributed industrial and other products.

This chapter records the stocks held by the sample of companies, their destocking during 1980/81 and the financial record of the companies. The source of data for these analyses was the published accounts of companies.

STOCKS

Table 7.1 sets out the reduction in total stocks held by the sample of companies in their latest accounting year. The change in the volume of total stocks held by the sample is shown in column 6, and the average percentage change in stocks is shown in column 7. The 17.5 per cent reduction in the volume of stocks held by the sample amounted to £1.2 billion at late 1980 prices. Eighty six per cent of the sales of the sample of companies were in the UK or were exports from the UK. Assuming the breakdown between UK and overseas stocks were the same as for sales, the reduction in UK stocks by the sample was £1,034 million. [3] This represented 32 per cent of the total estimated reduction in stocks in the economy in 1980 (according to the expenditure estimates of GDP made at the end of 1983) and 21 per cent of destocking between the end of June 1980 and June 1981. [4] These comparisons suggest that the sample accounted for about a quarter of the total destocking in the UK. [5]

The total and average changes in the volume of stocks, -17.5 and -20.2 per cent, are quite similar. The unweighted average is of interest because the sample included five of the ten largest UK manufacturing companies, but only a very small proportion of smaller companies. The large companies dominate the (weighted) aggregates. If the smaller companies in the sample are representative of other companies in their size range and below which destocked, then the unweighted average provides a useful alternative measure of changes in stocks. The comparison shows that destocking by the smaller companies in the sample was not very different from destocking by the giants.

The percentage run down of stocks by the sample of retail companies was nearly as sharp as that for manufacturing. This reflects the aggregate destocking by these industries during 1980 recorded in Table 3.1, retailers stocks fell by 5.7 per cent compared to a 6.4 per cent fall in stocks held by manufacturers.

Table 7.2 shows the distribution of rates of destocking by sample companies. The rapid run down of stocks by sample companies is not surprising as this was the criteria for selecting the sample.

Table 7.1. Stocks held by the sample of companies at the beginning and end of their accounting year. (a)

	Number of companies	Stocks at the: beginning of the year	end of the year	Cost of sales adjustment (b)	Percentage change: in stocks at at current prices (c)	in the volume of stocks (d) total	average
	(1)	(2)	(3)	(4)	(5)	(6)	(7)
Manufacturing (e)	26	4,825	4,255	320	-11.8	-17.3	-20.5
Retailing	10	856	771	62	-9.9	-16.0	-17.4
Distributors	6	690	627	103	-9.1	-20.9	-23.4
Total	42	6,370	5,643	485	-11.3	-17.5	-20.2

Source: the published accounts of sample companies.

(a) Ten companies - mainly retailers - had year ends at the end of January 1981, eight in December 1980, eleven in March 1981, and the rest of the sample in other months between October 1980 and August 1981.

(b) The cost of sales adjustment represents the difference between the historical cost of stocks consumed and their replacement cost at the time of use. It has been added to opening stocks to convert them to end of year prices.

(c) The percentage change between column (2) and column (3).

(d) The percentage change between (column (2) plus column (4)) and column (3).

(e) Companies were allocated to their main field of operation as measured by turnover.

Table 7.2
Destocking by the Sample of Companies

Type of Company	Percentage Reduction in the Volume of Stocks during Accounting Year: less than 10%	10.1 to 15%	15.1 to 20%	20.1 to 30%	30.1 to 40%	Total
	(Number of Companies)					
Manufacturing	1	5	10	8	2	26
Retailing	-	5	3	1	1	10
Distribution	-	1	1	3	1	6
Total	1	11	14	12	4	42

Source: the published accounts of sample companies.

THE FINANCIAL RECORD

One purpose of this section is to describe the financial position of the sample of companies during the period of destocking. The reasons companies gave for destocking are described in Chapter 8, they include reductions in profits and cash flow. There were three main sources of pressure on companies in 1980. The recession caused a fall in demand which reduced sales and product prices relative to costs, UK interest rates rose as part of a world wide increase and inflation was increasing the cost of replacing stocks. Here the reductions in profits and cash flow are recorded and the relative importance of the three pressures as causes of the reductions in profits and cash flow are assessed.

Table 7.3 summarises the financial record of the sample of manufacturing and retail companies for their two latest financial years, the year of destocking and the previous year. The accounting data are affected by inflation and the changing rate of inflation, and include the effects of the changes companies made in response to the recession and financial squeeze. Data for all the sample manufacturing and retail companies, and for these companies but excluding the giant companies, are shown. Attention is focused on the data for companies excluding the giants which are considered later. (The giants include British Leyland and British Steel whose

Table 7.3 Financial Record

(a) Sales, Stocks and Profits

	Manufacturing Companies				Retail Companies			
	All		Excluding five giants		All		Excluding three giants	
	1979/80	1980/81	1979/80	1980/81	1979/80	1980/81	1979/80	1980/81
	£m.							
Sales and Stocks								
1. World Sales	18,910	19,120	2,007	1,941	5,640	6,090	1,641	1,736
2. UK sales and exports	15,267	15,355	1,567	1,496	5,351	5,775	1,629	1,724
3. (UK sales and exports as % of world sales)	80.7	80.3	78.1	77.1	94.9	94.8	99.3	99.3
4. Stocks at end of year	4,824	4,255	539	454	856	771	273	231
5. (Stocks as % of world sales)	25.5	22.2	26.9	23.4	15.2	12.7	16.6	13.3
Profits								
Historical Accounting Profits[a]								
6. Trading profit[b]	660	-125	141	90	412	398	134	117
7. Less interest	-442	-525	-44	-55	-9	-26	-7	-6
8. Profit before taxation	218	-650	98	34	393	362	127	111
9. Less taxation	-197	-205	-27	-15	-127	-133	-33	-40
10. Profit after taxation	20	-855	71	19	266	229	94	70
11. Less dividends	-233	-175	-24	-19	-112	-108	-56	-50
12. Retained profits	-213	-1,030	48	0	155	120	40	19
13. Extraordinary items	-1,188	-753	-6	-30	19	-4	-8	-18

Table 7.3 continued

Inflation Adjusted Profits								
14. Extra depreciation	-375	-443	-23	-26	-28	-36	-11	-12
15. Adjustment for working capital financed with equity capital(c)	+22	+209	-28	-26	-86	-79	-27	-28
16. Inflation adjusted profit before taxation (Row 8 + Row 14 + Row 15)	-135	-884	47	-18	279	247	89	71

(a) The data are based on recorded costs. These are generally historical costs but fixed assets include revaluations and depreciation includes the effects of these revaluations.

(b) Trading profits are after deducting depreciation.

(c) The inflation adjustment for working capital financed with equity capital is described in the text.

Table 7.3 continued

(b) Cash Flow and Balance Sheets

Cash Flow	Manufacturing Companies				Retail Companies			
	All		Excluding five giants		All		Excluding five giants	
Sources	1979/80	1980/81	1979/80	1980/81	1979/80	1980/81	1979/80	1980/81
				£m.				
17. Profit before taxation	218	-650	98	34	393	362	127	111
18. Depreciation	576	661	50	58	66	85	17	21
19. Sales of fixed assets	144	167	31	18	43	79	35	20
20. Increase in creditors[h]	156	345	54	-48	154	31	64	3
21. Net increase in loans and deferred liabilities	20	3	42	25	4	51	6	-2
22. Issues of share capital	1,096	1,722	2	0	40	1	35	0
Total	2,210	2,249	276	88	700	609	284	153
Applications								
23. Taxation	185	106	23	23	34	42	43	47
24. Dividends	213	226	23	23	96	112	44	56
25. Purchases of fixed assets[h]	1,754	1,691	102	82	252	250	77	54
26. Increase in stocks[h]	423	-515	46	-74	156	-82	63	-35
27. Increase in debtors[h]	-83	341	49	-39	144	35	63	1
28. Payments to associated cos and for new subsidiaries[h]	33	23	29	8	88	80	-7	-16
29. Exceptional and extraordinary items[d]	3	562	14	38	8	9	1	7
Total	2,528	2,435	286	61	777	445	285	115
30. Balance being net inflow of cash (and reduction of overdrafts)	-318	-186	-10	+28	-76	+164	0	+38

Table 7.3 continued

Memorandum Items								
31. 16% on the reduction in stocks(e)		142		18		23		9
32. 4% on stocks held at the end of year	193	170	21	18	34	31	11	10
Balance Sheets								
33. Equity capital	6,234	6,137	665	677	2,096	2,201	710	703
34. Loan capital	3,581	3,484	176	201	124	170	79	72
35. Gearing ratio (line 34 as % of line 33)	57	57	26	30	6	8	11	10
36. Bank balances(f)	-547	-734	-88	-62	-31	+119	-10	+27
37. Gearing ratio (lines 34 - 36 as % of line 33)	66	69	40	39	7	2	13	6
38. Fixed assets at recorded costs	7,718	8,038	479	549	1,536	1,645	513	523
39. Current assets(h)	8,399	8,193	954	828	1,917	1,929	673	621
40. Current liabilities(g)(h)	5,456	5,815	547	466	1,166	1,143	391	366
41. Net current assets	2,942	2,378	406	363	750	786	282	255

(d) Extraordinary items included in the cash flow statment are not identical with those recorded in the profit and loss statement. For cash flow purposes extraordinary items involve cash outlay or receipts during the year. Some of the extraordinary items included in the profit and loss account are provisions. These provisions are excluded from exceptional and extraordinary items included in the cash flow statement.

(e) The reduction in stocks is the change in the volume of stocks calculated by using the cost of sales adjustment. It is not the change in the value of stocks shown in row 4.

(f) Bank balances are the differences between the sum of positive bank balances and the sum of short-term borrowing: some companies have positive balances, some overdrafts and some both.

(g) Current liabilities include creditors and short-term borrowing.

(h) The components of cash flow generally exclude assets and liabilities acquired by takeovers or assets of businesses which were sold during the year. The net effect of these transactions are included in row 28. The balance sheet data include assets and liabilities acquired by takeovers, and exclude the assets of business which were sold.

Source: The published accounts of sample companies.

results affect significantly the estimates for all manufacturing companies).

A glance at the recorded, historical, financial data indicates the severity of the pressures on manufacturing companies. Already in 1979/80 manufacturing companies were less profitable (in relation to sales and equity capital) and were more highly geared than the retail companies. In 1980/81 trading profits measured in historical costs of the manufacturing companies (shown in row 6) fell by 36 per cent, compared to a fall of 13 per cent for retailers, [6] and the extraordinary write offs by manufacturers were greater. In real terms the fall in recorded trading profits was steeper; retail prices rose by 18 per cent between 1979 and 1980. Recorded profits of the sample of manufacturing companies fell by 46 per cent in real terms.

INFLATION ADJUSTED PROFITS [7]

So far the comparisons have been based upon the historical accounting data. Do they present a misleading view of the change in profits because of distortions caused by inflation? Charles Kennedy has described the alternative definitions of inflation adjusted profits. [8] Here the profit attributable to the owners of the equity of companies is considered. The equity capital of a company has to be maintained in real terms before a company can claim to show a profit for the owners of the equity in the company. Rows 14 to 16 of Table 7.3 show the adjustment of pre-tax profits for inflation. There are two adjustments, relating to the ownership of fixed assets and of net current assets. Underlying the adjustments is an assumption that equity capital finances fixed assets and any balance remaining contributes to financing net current assets. Reasons for adopting this assumption are described below.

The adjustment of depreciation of fixed assets for inflation in row 14 is based on the adjustments made by companies for their current cost accounts. [9] It is assumed that their current cost depreciation charges would maintain the real value of fixed assets. The adjustment is the difference between current and historical cost depreciation. The second adjustment shown in row 15 is for current assets financed with equity capital. It is based on the book value of the equity capital less the book value of fixed assets at the beginning of the accounting year - equity capital which is not used to finance fixed assets is used to finance net current assets. The national income deflator for total final expenditure was used to calculate this adjustment. [10] The adjustment for manufacturing companies excluding the giants, and those for retail companies are negative, these companies finance a part of their net current assets with equity capital. The adjustments show the profit, including stock appreciation, required to maintain the real value of these current assets. [11] The adjustment for all manufacturing companies (including the giant companies) is positive because on balance the giant manufacturing companies do not finance any of their current assets out of equity capital, and a part of their fixed assets is financed by borrowing. The positive adjustment is for the gain these companies obtain by the reduction in the real value of their borrowing to finance fixed assets.

The important points about the inflation adjusted profits are that they are lower than historical cost profits, and that the inflation adjusted profits were lower in 1980/81 than in 1979/80, as were profits measured in historical cost terms. The fall in profits shown by historical accounting data is not misleading.

CASH FLOW

The inward flow of cash and credit for manufacturing companies (excluding the giants) shown in part (b) of Table 7.3, dwindled in 1980/81. Apart from depreciation which increased, cash flow from each source fell. Profits before taxation fell by 64 per cent and the liabilities to creditors declined by £48 million in 1980/81, in contrast to a rise of £54 million in 1979/80. This change is reflected in the application of funds section. As companies reduced their stocks, their liabilities to creditors shrank. If destocking is achieved by reducing purchases there is no initial impact on cash flow; liabilities to creditors as well as stocks fall.

In spite of the decline in profits of the manufacturing companies, cash outflow for taxation and dividends was maintained. Purchases of fixed assets - investment - fell by 20 per cent. These three items are subject to lags. Taxes and dividends paid in a year relate to profits earned during earlier years, and much of the investment in 1980/81 was decided upon during the preceding years. Debtors fell by £39m with declining sales, but the cash outflow for exceptional and extraordinary items increased. However, the net result, shown in row 30, was a net cash inflow of £28 million. In summary the decline in profits between the two years and the increase in exceptional and extraordinary expenditure reduced the cash flow of companies. In the face of this reduction in cash flow, companies reduced debtors and stocks, and, though this was in part offset by a reduction in creditors, the net effect was a cash inflow. The decline in both the cash inflow and outflow for retailers was milder than for manufacturers. They also had a net cash inflow, of £38 million in 1980/81.

The giant manufacturing companies had a net outflow of cash in both years. Although the net outflow of cash for 'all the manufacturing companies' fell from £318 million in 1979/80 to £186 million in 1980/81, this was after a much increased infusion of equity capital for the nationalised giant companies. The pressure on the cash flow of 'all manufacturing companies' originated with the reduction in trading profits, a turn round from +£218 million to -£650 million, and an increase in their cash outflow for exceptional and extraordinary items from £3 million to £562 million.

BALANCE SHEETS [12]

Balance sheet information for the samples of companies is summarised in Table 7.3(b). This is in terms of historical costs because the current cost estimates of fixed assets published in company accounts do not provide a satisfactory guide to the value of plant and machinery. Although the replacement cost of these assets was increasing, some of them would not be replaced if they were lost, and those which would be replaced would not be replaced with identical equipment. Another reason for using historical cost data is that financial analysts generally estimate gearing ratios in historical cost terms.

The loan plus bank borrowing to equity capital gearing ratio for manufacturing companies, excluding the giants, shown in row 37, improved slightly in 1980/81, but their net current assets which are shown in row 41, shrank. The same gearing ratio for retail companies which were in a strong position to borrow because of their property assets, was much lower than for the manufacturers.

Table 7.4 gives another presentation of the recorded accounting results of companies. Here the profits and other variables for each company are taken as a percentage of its world wide sales in 1980/81, and the results averaged. This procedure gives an equal weight to each company regardless of its size. Again the effects of the recession are shown to have been sharper for the manufacturers.

Table 7.4 Profits, Interest and Cash Flow as Percentages of Sales in 1980/81 (a)

	Companies							
	Manufacturers		Retailers		Distributors		All	
	1979/80	1980/81	1979/80	1980/81	1979/80	1980/81	1979/80	1980/81
1. Number of companies	26		10		6		42	
Profits				(unweighted averages)				
2. Trading profits	5.9	3.1	6.7	6.0	9.9	8.5	6.7	4.6
3. Interest	-1.9	-2.2	+0.2	+0.1	-0.7	-1.1	-1.2	-1.5
4. Profit before tax	4.0	0.9	6.9	6.1	9.2	7.4	5.5	3.1
5. Profit after tax and dividends	1.7	-1.3	2.5	1.5	4.1	2.9	2.2	0.0
6. The cost of sales adjustment	-	1.4	-	1.0	-	1.3	-	1.3

(a) The percentages are based on recorded cost data.

Source: the published accounts of sample companies.

TRADING PROFITS AND INTEREST PAYMENTS

An important comparison is between the fall in trading profits, an indicator of the impact of the recession on the cash flow of companies, and the increase in interest payments, an indicator of the direct effects of the monetary squeeze on cash flow.

The decline in recorded cost trading profits for manufacturers was much greater than the increase in interest payments (rows 6 and 7 of Table 7.3 and rows 2 and 3 of Table 7.4). Trading profits of twenty two of the sample of twenty six manufacturing companies fell, and for all but one of these companies the fall in trading profits exceeded the increase in actual interest payments. The average fall in trading profits as a percentage of sales between 1979/80 and 1980/81 was 2.1 percentage points for all the companies, and the increase in interest payments averaged 0.3 per cent (Table 7.4).

The increase in interest payments occurred inspite of decisions to cut borrowing by destocking and other means. A guide to the pressure on cash flow stemming from high interest rates per se in the latest year, is to take a proportion, say, a quarter of interest payments in the penultimate year as an indicator of unusually high interest rates. That would be 0.5 per cent of sales for manufactures, (25 per cent of 1.9 per cent (row 3, column 1 of Table 7.4)). Again the pressure on cash flow is much smaller than that caused by the fall in trading profits of 2.8 percentage points between 1979/80 and 1980/81.

The third pressure on cash flow was caused by inflation; stocks were replaced at increasing prices. The size of this requirement for additional working capital is indicated by the cost of sales adjustment shown in row 7 of Table 7.4, which averaged 1.3 per cent of sales for all companies. During 1980/81 wholesale prices rose less rapidly than during 1979/80, [13] so there was some moderation of the demand for additional working capital to finance stocks attributable to inflation, but substantial extra finance would have been required in 1980/81 if the volume of stocks had not been reduced. [14]

STOCKS AND INTEREST

Other indicators of destocking and interest charges are shown in Table 7.3. Row 31 shows the potential effects of destocking - the reduction in physical stocks - on interest payments (or receipts) in a full year. For this purpose an interest rate of 16 per cent was used, representative of the rates applicable in 1980. For manufacturers excluding the giants, the effect of destocking on interest charges represents about a quarter of the reduction in profits before taxation. [15]

FINANCING STOCKS

The importance of the source of finance (equity, loans or credit from suppliers) for stockholding was underlined in the debate about stock relief described at the beginning of Chapter 5. Companies do not have to relate sources of finance to their uses. Retained profits, depreciation provisions, borrowing and the proceeds of new issues of equity capital, provide a pool of resources to meet demands for financing investments and working capital. One approach would be to relate the sources of the stock of funds employed to uses in proportion to the ratio of the contributions of the source of funds employed to total funds employed. This assumes that each category of funds is applied to uses in the same proportion as its contribution to total funds employed. This approach is not realistic because, in general, firms cannot finance fixed investment with trade credit or short term bank loans. An alternative approach is to assume that equity capital finances fixed assets first, and that any residual equity finances stocks then other net current assets. Loan capital is the second most permanent source of capital in terms of liquidity, and bank borrowing and credit from suppliers follow; they finance the holding of assets so far as they are not financed from equity and loan capital. In this way both sides of a company's balance sheet are matched in terms of liquidity.

For all the sets of companies distinguished, equity and loan capital together exceeded fixed assets at book value, so some capital was left to finance stocks. For manufacturing companies excluding the giants, the residual equity capital (equity capital, including reserves, less fixed assets) represented 35 per cent of stocks and for retailers 72 per cent in 1979/80. Loan capital represented 33 per cent of stocks for manufacturers. These figures are based on aggregates and they mask wide differences in financing between the companies included in the samples.

THE GIANTS

Table 7.5 presents the financial record of seven of the giant companies included in the sample. The high stocks to sales ratio (shown in row 5) for the two nationalised manufacturing companies, British Leyland and British Steel, were notable;

Table 7.5 Financial Record (Giant Companies)

Recorded (Historical Cost) Data

	ICI & Courtaulds		British Leyland & British Steel		Three Giant Retailers	
	1979/80	1980/81	1979/80	1980/81	1979/80	1980/81
			£m			
Sales and Stocks						
World sales	7,187	7,425	6,095	5,831	3,999	4,354
U.K. sales + exports	4,890	4,965	5,595	5,337	3,722	4,051
U.K. sales + exports as % of world sales	68	67	92	92	93	93
Stocks end of year	1,576	1,409	2,208	1,909	583	540
Stocks as % of world sales	22	19	36	33	14.6	12.4
Profits						
Trading profit	746	388	-407	-783	278	281
less interest	-106	-140	-254	-277	-12	-30
	639	249	-661	-1,059	266	251
less taxation	-143	-135	-14	-9	94	93
Profit after taxation	496	114	-676	-1,069	172	159
less dividends	158	104	0	0	56	58
Retained profits	338	10	-676	-1,069	116	101
Extraordinary items	-43	-248	-1,253	-487	1	32

Table 7.5 continued

Balance Sheets.						
Equity capital	3,250	3,067	1,533	1,656	1,386	1,498
Loan capital	1,445	1,589	1,690	1,431	45	98
Gearing ratio (loan capital)	44	52	110	86	3	7
Bank balances[f]	+173	+232	-494	-615	-21	+92
Gearing ratio (loan capital and bank balance)	39	44	142	124	5	0
Fixed assets at recorded costs	3,549	3,833	2,598	2,568	1,023	1,122
Current assets	3,505	3,355	3,078	3,127	1,244	1,308
Current liabilities[g]	1,793	1,822	2,413	2,558	775	777
Net current assets	1,712	1,533	665	568	468	531

Source: the published accounts of companies.

The footnotes are the same as for Table 7.3.

stocks represented a third of sales even after destocking in 1980/81.

Again the fall in trading profits and increase in trading losses of the manufacturing giants swamp the increases in interest payments.

QUARTERLY DATA

So far all the comparisons of profitability have been between the two accounting years. Companies were not asked to provide quarterly stocks and profits data. The published quarterly breakdown of profits for I.C.I. reproduced in Table 7.6, shows an alarming profits slide during 1980. From our discussions with managers of other manufacturing companies, it was clear that some of them had a similar experience. The first quarter of 1980 was good, but there was an abrupt decline in demand about April 1980. [16]

Table 7.6
ICI's Sales and Profits before Tax

	Sales[(a)]		Profits before tax	
	1979	1980	1979	1980
Q_1	1,185(100)	1,523(105)	98	162
Q_2	1,382(109)	1,452 (98)	162	80
Q_3	1,326(100)	1,304 (86)	155	-10
Q_4	1,475(108)	1,436 (95)	145	-6

(a) The figures in brackets are a volume index based on I.C.I.'s sales figures and the wholesale price index for the output of the chemical and allied industries.

Source: I.C.I's Annual Report for 1980.

CONCLUSIONS

A principal purpose of the comparisons of financial data was to assess the relative importance to companies of the recession and the financial squeeze, particularly the effects of high interest rates. The comparisons shown in Table 7.3 and 7.4 demonstrate the predominance of the impact of the recession for the sample of manufacturing companies. For retailers the effects of the recession on profits and cash flow were less sharp than for manufacturers, but so were the effects of high interest rates on interest payments.

NOTES

[1] One manufacturing company with sales of less than £20 million was included at the start of the enquiry before the size rule was established.

[2] Giant companies were defined as companies with sales including VAT of more than £1 billion.

[3] In fact UK stocks were reduced more than overseas stocks. (Evidence obtained from the sample of companies).

[4] The distribution of year ends for the sample is summarised in footnote (a) to Table 7.1; they centred on January and February 1981. The year ends of the giant companies included in the sample were concentrated on December 1980 and January 1981.

[5] Some companies increased their stocks so the total destocking by companies which destocked was greater than the net destocking by all companies taken together.

[6] Trading profits are the trading profits reported by companies plus profits attributable to minority interests.

[7] Wynne Godley and Francis Cripps have described an accounting framework to analyse the effects of inflation on company finance in 'Macroeconomics' OUP 1983.

[8] Charles Kennedy: 'Inflation Accounting: Retrospect and Prospect', CEPG Review, March 1978.

[9] 'Current cost' estimates of profits were not made for both accounting years by nearly half the companies included in the sample. For companies which did not estimate current cost profits, the depreciation adjustment was assumed to be the same in relation to their historical depreciation charge as for the sample companies which did estimate the adjustment.

[10] For the year of destocking the average change in the deflator between the 4th Q of 1979 and the 4th Q of 1980, and between the 1st Q of 1980 and the 1st Q of 1981, 14.1 per cent, was used. For the preceding year the deflator was 17.5 per cent.

[11] No inflation adjustment is made for current assets financed out of borrowing including trade credit. Stock appreciation is included in profits and the effects of inflation on assets and liabilities cancel out.

[12] Some of the balance sheet data does not tie in with data in the earlier sections of Table 7.3. For example, exchange rate adjustments affect the figures for loans and fixed assets shown in the balance sheets, but as they do not affect cash flow they are not included in the cash flow statement. Also the cash flow data for changes in fixed assets, stocks, debtors and creditors exclude acquisitions and sales of businesses. The balance sheet data for assets and liabilities include assets and liabilities acquired by acquisition.

[13] Between January 1979 and January 1980 the index of wholesale prices of materials bought by manufacturing industry rose by 27 per cent and of output by 18 per cent. During the following year the increases were 8 and 11 per cent.

[14] For companies with taxable profits, stock relief would finance about half of any increase in the value of stocks.

[15] In practice the effect of destocking during 1980 on interest payments in that year was much less because destocking was spread through the year not concentrated at the beginning, and because at first destocking had little impact on cash flow as it was offset by a reduction in liabilities to creditors. Row 32 of Table 7.3 shows a charge of four per cent on stocks, four per cent is taken as representative of the real rate of interest paid by large companies in normal circumstances. This charge for manufacturers represented 0.9 per cent of sales in 1979/80, and for retailers 0.6 per cent.

[16] For several companies the trend of business was confused by the steel strike. For example, the possibility of a shortage of tin cans caused buyers to stock up with paint during the strike and led to a fall in demand when the steel strike ended in May, 1980.

8 Evidence from the industrial enquiry on the causes of destocking

In this chapter the evidence about destocking and the explanations for destocking obtained from companies which destocked are described.

THE MANAGEMENT OF STOCKS

There were immense differences between companies in the range of goods held in stock and the extent to which stocks could be controlled from the centre of a group of companies. One subsidiary of a division of one public company held 80,000 different parts in stock for the textile machinery it manufactured, and it had an end of year stock to annual sales ratio of 0.4. Managers at the subsidiary company decided what stocks of parts and materials to hold. When planning stock levels they forecast sales of products and spare parts, and allowed for differences in costs for manufacturing different batch sizes, for different rates of utilisation of factory capacity and for varying rates of machine loading. At the other extreme, managers at the head office of a company which manufactured furniture could control stocks closely. The company had an end of year stocks to annual sales ratio of 0.07. It held only a few days supply of foam and timber and could manufacture short production runs with little cost disadvantage. Similarly a company operating a national chain of shops selling durable goods, controlled stocks from its head office through a small group of buyers aided by a computerised stock control system, and had a stock to annual sales ratio of 0.15.

Most of the manufacturing companies in the sample operated through a divisional and/or subsidiary company structure. The structure of the distribution companies was similar to that of the manufacturing companies, but the retailing companies were controlled from the centre; generally goods were ordered from suppliers by buyers at the head office, and stocks held at stores were monitored in detail at the head office.

The stocks held by most companies were not at optimum levels calculated in a precise way in relation to expected sales, delivery and production lead times, estimates of the chances of disruption to supplies or production, rates of inflation and interest rates. Levels of actual stocks were the result of decisions taken by managers based on their judgement, and events such as actual sales diverging from expected sales.

At the beginning of each year a company starts with a level of stocks. Future levels of planned stocks emerge through a process of budgeting and discussion between managers and accountants at subsidiaries and those at the group head office. The control variable central planners and financial staff use is the stocks to sales ratio. [1] Deviations of the actual ratios from the budgeted ratios, or budgeted ratios compared to past actual ratios, especially increasing ratios, trigger questioning of managers of operating companies.

The relative influence of the managers and planners at head office and at subsidiaries varies between companies. Also the influence of different groups varies with circumstances. Decisions made by managers of a subsidiary which is profitable are less likely to be challenged. When sales and profits are buoyant production and selling departments may be allowed to increase stocks in line with optimistic sales forecasts and to ensure that orders can be met.

Managers adapt to events. Either while planning for 1980/81 or during the year, many managements decided to reduce stocks. [2] One clear and important, though unsurprising, result of the enquiry was to find that for many companies there were a number of forces exerting pressure for a reduction of stocks. In these circumstances managers do not allot to each pressure for reducing stocks a target reduction in stocks. A decision is made to reduce stocks in response to a whole set of events.

CATEGORIES OF STOCKS

Only for manufacturing is the division into categories of

stocks, raw materials, work in progress and finished goods, relevant. But even for most companies operating in manufacturing industry, the main focus of attention is total stocks. In the first instance managers deal with the total stocks to sales ratio not the ratios for categories of stocks to sales.

Among the sample of manufacturing companies, the fall in stocks was much sharper for raw material stocks than finished goods. Excluding the giants, the weighted fall at recorded book prices was 25 per cent for raw materials, 15 per cent for work in progress and six per cent for finished goods. [3] The equivalent average or unweighted percentage falls were 22, 18 and ten. The intense destocking of raw materials by the sample tallies well with the pattern of destocking for manufacturing industry shown in Table 6.1. The run down of work in progress by the sample was faster than for manufacturing industry in total.

RATIO OF STOCKS TO EXPECTED SALES

One focus of the enquiry was to split the change in stocks between the change in stocks proportional to the change in the expected volume of sales, and the change in the stocks to expected sales ratio. Table 8.1 shows the average change in the expected volume of sales and the stocks to expected sales ratio for companies in the sample. For many companies, budgeted sales in the first quarter of the year following the latest accounting year were compared with those for the same quarter of the preceding year, to provide a guide to the change in expected sales. For some engineering companies a longer time span was required for estimating the stocks to sales ratio because the lead time and production cycle were longer.

The striking result of the comparisons in Table 8.1 is the decline in the stocks to expected sales ratio. For the sample as a whole, the unweighted average decline in the stocks to expected sales ratio was 12 per cent; the decline for the sample of manufacturing companies was also 12 per cent, and for retailing companies 13 per cent. The unweighted average decline in the expected volume of sales for the whole sample was 12 per cent. For the manufacturing companies the aggregate and unweighted average falls in the expected volume of sales were sharp, 13 per cent.

	Number of Companies[a]	Percentage Change in Volume of Stocks		Percentage Change in the Volume of Expected Sales		Percentage Change in the Stocks/Expected Sales Ratio	
		Weighted(b)	Unweighted	Weighted(b)	Unweighted	Weighted(b)	Unweighted
Manufacturing	23	-19	-24	-13	-13	-7	-12
Retailing	9	-15	-16	-4	-4	-11	-13
Distribution	6	-22	-24	-19	-14	-3	-11
Total	38	-19	-22	-13	-11	-7	-12

(a) Estimates of changes in expected sales were not obtained for three manufacturing companies and one retail company.

(b) Weighted by stocks.

Table 8.2 shows the distribution of expected changes in the volume of sales. [4] Managers of some companies had great difficulty forecasting sales because of uncertainty about market developments. [5] Even for a company as large as ICI, trading conditions changed very quickly in 1980 as shown in Table 7.6. Also there were problems in calculating the expected volume of sales because of price adjustments. [6]

Most of the firms in the sample based their expectations of future sales on current experience in, and knowledge of, the markets they served. There seemed little disposition by manufacturers to formulate a model of how the economy as a whole operates and how their markets would be affected by changes in the economy. Although many manufacturers are affected by movements of the economy, the timing of the effects of changes in the economy varies for individual businesses, and this explains why managers concentrate on developments in their own markets. Some retail companies took a closer interest in movements of the economy, perhaps because changes affect them earlier than manufacturers. Also the business of manufacturers is more specialised than that of most retailers. [7]

There are qualifications to the estimates of changes in expected sales and the stocks to sales ratios in Tables 8.1 and 8.2. For some companies, the comparisons were for parts of their operations, and for some companies the comparisons were affected by take overs or disposals. Some companies provided a guide to the change in the expected volume of sales e.g. that the change was small. These were used to make numerical estimates. Nevertheless the implication that many companies in the sample reduced stocks faster than they expected sales to fall is a firm one, although the average figures are not very reliable. [8]

Table 8.2 Expected Percentage Change in the Volume of Sales between the end of 1979/80 and the end of 1980/81.

	Total	-10% or more	-5% and less than 9.9%	0 to 4.9%	0.1 to 5.0%	5.1% or more
			(number of companies)			
Manufacturing	23	15	6	1	0	1
Retailing	9	1	3	4	1	0
Distribution	6	5	0	1	0	0
Total	38	21	9	6	1	1

It cannot be assumed that the change in stocks attributable to the change in expected sales and the change in stocks attributable to other factors, are caught in the percentage change in the volume of expected sales, and the percentage change in the stocks to expected sales ratio. A priori reasons for expecting the stocks to sales ratio to move in either direction as a consequence of a fall in expected sales were given in Chapter 4. Prior to the enquiry I would have expected that, on balance, the fall in planned stocks would be rather less than a fall in the volume of expected sales, in the absence of other changes affecting stocks. So the fact that the stocks to expected sales ratio fell substantially would have indicated there were other powerful forces contributing to destocking besides the fall in demand. However, from the enquiry it is clear that the relationship between stocks and sales is flexible for most companies. An adverse event such as a fall in expected sales, can precipitate a reduction in stocks <u>and</u> the stocks to sales ratio. In addition there are indirect effects of a fall in demand on profits and cash flow which may lead to reductions in stocks.

EXPECTED AND ACTUAL SALES

In Table 8.3 changes in the volume of actual sales are compared to the changes in expected sales. The comparisons are based on changes in actual sales between successive first <u>halves</u> of companies' accounting years. (Data for half years were used because most companies do not publish quarterly turnover data). These comparisons suggest that the manufacturers under estimated the decline in sales, and retail companies underestimated the buoyancy of sales, but the latter conclusion is qualified. [9] Although the average of the expected and actual sales for the sample are in close accord, there were wide divergencies for some companies.

These comparisons show that destocking was faster than the decline in actual sales, as well as faster than the decline in expected sales. The fact that companies reduced their stocks to sales ratios shows that there are two questions to answer, why firms had the scope for reducing their stocks to sales ratios and what caused them to do so? The reduction in the stocks to sales ratio does not necessarily mean that companies held 'excess' stocks, the reduction could be achieved by, for example, closing businesses with above average stocks to sales ratios or by introducing new lines with low stocks to sales ratios.

Table 8.3 The Change in Actual Sales

	Number of Companies	Unweighted Percentage change in actual sales first half 1979/80 to first half 1980/81 in volume terms(a)	Unweighted Percentage change in the volume of expected sales first quarter 1979/80 to the first quarter 1980/81
Manufacturing	22	-17	-13
Retailing	7	-1	-6
Distribution	4	0	-12
Total	33	-12	-11

(a) Sales figures published by companies were adjusted for changes in prices. Wholesale prices were used to adjust sales of manufacturing companies and retail prices to adjust sales of retail companies.

Another complication for disentangling the causes of destocking is that a reason for having high stocks may not explain a subsequent reduction. For example, a reversal of tax incentives to hold extra stocks need not trigger a reduction in stocks held to take advantage of the tax rules. A reduction in demand causing a reduction in profits and cash flow could do so.

EXPLANATIONS FOR DESTOCKING

The reasons managers gave for destocking are listed in Table 8.4. The reasons for destocking emerged as answers to a series of questions put to managers at interviews. A check list of these questions is shown in Appendix B. Terms such as profitability and cash flow were not defined, but managers did not require clarification of these terms. The main difficulty was to pinpoint the causes of destocking where a number of inter related factors combined to influence and trigger a run down of stocks. Managers were also asked the three most important causes of destocking. Their answers are summarised in Table 8.5.

Table 8.4

The Pressures for and Causes of Destocking apart from a fall in expected sales.

	Manufacturing		Retailing		Distribution		Total	
	Yes	No	Yes	No	Yes	No	Yes	No
1. High interest rates	12	13	7	3	1	5	20	21
2. Cash flow squeeze	13	11	2	8	2	4	17	23
3. Gearing limits	9	15	1	9	1	5	11	29
4. Profits squeeze	15	7	7	3	2	4	24	14
5. Slower inflation - direct	8	15	0	10	4	2	12	27
6. - indirect (allowing slack)	9	11	3	7	2	2	14	20
7. Easier of supply	4	9	2	5	4	1	10	15
8. Tax rules - direct	7	18	4	6	3	2	14	26
9. - indirect (allowing slack)	8	16	2	7	3	2	13	25
10. Write downs	5	13	0	5	2	2	7	20
11. Special factors (a)	15	9	6	2	3	2	24	13
12. Closures and disposals	16	8	2	8	3	3	21	19
13. Rationalisation	10	13	2	8	0	6	12	27
14. Changes in product range	6	15	0	10	0	6	6	31

(a) Some companies gave more than one special factor. The most common special factor was that the company was overstocked at the end of the previous year for reasons other than obtaining tax relief on stocks or because of expected rapid inflation. This applied to eight companies, including three where the slack had built up over some years rather than occurring in the previous year alone. Five companies reduced stocks because of measures to increase efficiency. These included the use of a new warehouse and the introduction of a more effective cash control system. Other special factors included a fire, loss of control of stocks at a subsidiary, a switch to North Sea oil from imported oil, a change of strategy about maintaining output and employment at the clothing factories operated by a retail chain, redundant stocks acquired by takeover, the effects of strikes (two companies) and the appointment of a Chairman with new ideas.

Table 8.5 The Main Pressures for and Causes of Destocking

(number of companies)

		Reduction in Demand	Cash Flow Squeeze	Profits Squeeze	Closures and Disposals	Tax Rules	Interest Rates	Slower Inflation	Gearing Limits	Other or Special Factors
Manufacturing	1st	13	4	1	2	4	0	0	1	1
	2nd	5	5	3	2	2	1	0	1	5
	3rd	5	1	3	3	0	2	2	1	7
Retailing	1st	4	0	0	1	1	1	0	0	3
	2nd	3	0	0	0	0	0	1	0	0
	3rd	1	0	3	0	0	1	1	0	2
Distribution	1st	3	0	0	0	1	0	0	0	2
	2nd	2	0	1	1	1	0	0	0	2
	3rd	0	2	0	0	0	0	0	0	2
Total	1st	20	4	1	3	6	1	0	1	6
	2nd	10	5	4	3	3	5	1	1	7
	3rd	6	3	6	3	0	2	3	1	11
	1 to 3	36	12	11	9	9	8	4	3	24

QUALIFICATIONS

Some of the questions were 'sensitive'; piling up stocks to take advantage of tax relief is not illegal, but companies which announced they were adding to their stocks to obtain relief might lose the relief. Nor would managers of a company readily admit that it was up against externally imposed gearing limits.

Another qualification to the answers summarised in Tables 8.4 and 8.5 is that they are not always given by the managers who made the decisions to destock or not all the managers who contributed to the decisions. Nevertheless most of the managers with whom destocking was discussed were in a very good position to assess the forces leading to destocking and many of them took a prominent part in the decision making process. In 1980/81 decisions to reduce stocks were taken at senior management levels.

LESS IMPORTANT FACTORS

Tables 8.4 and 8.5 do make it possible to dispose of some factors as major causes of destocking. In combination the tables show that rationalisation and changes to product ranges were not substantial explanations. [10] Twelve out of thirty nine companies and six out of thirty seven companies respectively, regarded these as factors in destocking, but no company gave them as a main reason.

Fewer companies were asked about write downs, but only a third of these companies recognised it as a factor. [11] Only one company gave it as a main factor, and for the companies which quantified the effects of write downs, the contribution to destocking was small. For three companies write downs accounted for about ten per cent of the reduction in stocks and for the others much less. For the sample, average write downs represented about one per cent of the fall in the volume of stocks.

INFLATION

Two other forces, slower inflation and easier availability of goods, are shown by the responses summarised in Tables 8.4 and 8.5 to be factors contributing to destocking, but not factors of prime importance. Slower inflation affected stockholding in two ways. Some companies make a practice of buying certain products ahead of announced or expected price rises. For example, a paint manufacturer bought certain chemicals ahead of price rises which were announced in advance by the two suppliers. These extra stocks would be raw materials. Over the sample as a whole this type of stockbuilding and any change caused by slower inflation were claimed to be small. No company gave slower inflation as the main cause of destocking. [12]

Slower inflation had another impact on stock levels. Inflation had justified loose stock control for some companies or senior management had turned a blind eye to the build-up of stocks. During the ten years up to, and including, 1979, stocks had been a good hedge against inflation. In this sense, many companies including nearly half the manufacturers, did recognise slower inflation as a factor in a build up of stocks and the subsequent reduction in stocks.

EASIER AVAILABILITY OF SUPPLIES

Easier availability of supplies because of the recession was a factor which operated like slower inflation. It was a reason why managers were willing to be tough about stocks in 1980 and 1981, but no company gave it as a main reason for reducing stocks. Some retailers claimed that supplies were not more readily available because manufacturers had cut back their capacity. It could be that the interviews reported here under stress the effects of easier availability. Most of the interviews were with head office staff. Readier availability may have been a factor making it easier for managers of the subsidiaries of manufacturing companies and buyers of retail companies to comply with head office directives or pleas to reduce stocks without disrupting production or losing sales.

Rather late on in the enquiry the extent of stockbuilding ahead of shortages caused by strikes was examined. Certainly for some firms this had been an important factor. [13] In the steel and motor industries strikes led to a piling up of supplies and components.

THE REDUCTION IN DEMAND

Table 8.5 indicates the prime direct importance of the reduction in demand for destocking by all three groups. Nearly half the sample of companies which destocked gave it as the main cause of destocking and two thirds as the main or second most important factor. For the manufacturing companies for which the decline in demand was not one of the two main causes of destocking, the reasons were that the companies had a strong product range and/or were very competitive for other reasons, or that other reasons, a cash crisis, changes in tax rules, a decision to cut into the slack in stocks which was known to exist, were more important.

The description of the forces causing destocking given in Appendix E indicates that for retail companies the recession, or absence of the growth of demand, started in the autumn of 1979, while for many manufacturers it was not until the second quarter of 1980 that they felt the recession. The difference in the timing of decisions to destock supports the view that it was the decline in demand which triggered destocking because changes in external financial variables affected all trades simultaneously.

Direct competition from imports or the competition of imports for customer industries was important for about two thirds of the manufacturing companies for which a decline in demand was one of the two most important factors causing a decline in stocks. In other cases competition from imports was limited.

PROFITS AND CASH FLOW

Table 8.5 also shows the importance of three influences which were related to the fall in demand, the profits squeeze, the cash flow squeeze and closures. The extent of the fall in profits and cash flow have been recorded in Chapter 7. Profits were squeezed by the decline in demand and rising costs and interest rates. The decline in profits caused by the fall in demand, reduced cash flow. A decline in demand also has direct effects on cash flow. These are favourable at first for many firms as debtors pay their debts and purchases are cut back, but a reduction in wage costs through redundancies involves cash outlay, and many costs are difficult to cut in proportion to sales. The adverse effects of a recession on cash flow build up.

More than sixty per cent of companies faced a profits squeeze which acted as a pressure to reduce stocks, and for half of the manufacturing companies decisions to destock were influenced by a squeeze on their cash flow (Table 8.4). In terms of the main pressures for a reduction in stocks (Table 8.5) the profits squeeze and particularly cash flow squeeze were more important for manufacturers than for retailers and distributors. This corresponds to the smaller falls in profits and cash flow for retailers recorded in Chapter 7.

Close monitoring of cash flow is an important element of the control of the activities of divisions and subsidiaries by head offices. This is understandable for companies which are up against gearing limits or have shrinking profits, but it also applies to many other companies. Managers have learned from experience that monitoring and control of cash flow is one of the most effective means of controlling operating businesses in many industries. For most businesses reducing stocks is the only way to improve cash flow quickly, even though the initial impact of destocking on cash flow is offset by a decline in the amount owed to creditors.

Automatic pressure on cash flow as demand and profits fell caused businesses to reduce stocks, and these pressures were reinforced by the central managements of many companies. Alternative options for increasing cash flow were to slow payment of debts and to increase pressure on customers to speed up payment of their accounts. Although many companies tried to improve cash flow by measures of this type, most found that similar attempts by other firms offset their own measures. [14]

CLOSURES

Another response to the reduction in demand, profits squeeze and cash flow squeeze was to sell off businesses, and close factories and/or warehouses. In some cases product lines were sold off or abandoned, or were transferred to other factories or warehouses. [15]

INTEREST RATES

The theoretical impact of high interest rates on stock levels was described in Chapter 4. In practice it was money rates of interest rather than real rates which managers considered. One reason for this approach is that calculation of current real interest rates requires estimation of the rate of inflation. Also the rate of inflation of prices for products varies widely, so managers relate the expected increases in prices for the products they deal in to the rate of interest, rather than calculate a real rate of interest based on the rate of inflation in the economy as a whole, to use for planning purposes. In practice interest rates affected destocking in two ways. The direct effect was to induce firms to hold lower stocks by taking smaller deliveries, greater risks of being unable to meet orders, etc. As stated earlier most companies simply did not make calculations of the optimum level of stocks in which the interest rate was included. A few firms reported test calculations with interest rates. [16] Only six companies including three retailers, acknowledged that higher interest rates had a direct effect to reduce stocks. Two of the retailers reduced stocks to increase the interest they would earn on extra funds invested in the money market.

The practice of companies about charging interest is relevant to the effects of high rates of interest. Sixty per cent of the manufacturing companies which answered a question about charging subsidiaries interest did so. In most cases the subsidiaries were charged market rates on the changes in funds employed. [17] However, there are companies, including some giants, which do not charge their divisions and subsidiaries interest. Managers at the head office of these companies take account of interest rates when allocating funds and setting targets for cash flow.

The second effect of high interest rates was to cut into the profits of companies. It has been shown in Chapter 7 that the decline in trading profits was generally much greater than the effects of high interest rates on the profits of companies. However interest payments took 31 per cent of trading profits in the year before destocking took place. [18] Increases in interest rates at a time when trading profits were shrinking was a second blow for companies. Seventeen companies claimed that the impact of high interest rates on profits was a cause of destocking and twenty four that high interest rates did not have this effect.

Another view of the importance of interest rates for destocking is given by the analysis of the main reasons for destocking in Table 8.5. Only one company gave interest rates as the main reason for its destocking, four as the second main cause, and three as the third. Five out of eight of the positive responses were from retailers. Generally the reduction in demand was less for retailers. This suggests that if other pressures had not induced destocking by manufacturers, it is possible that high interest rates would have done so.

GEARING LIMITS

The other potential external monetary pressure was the availability of finance. The responses summarised in Tables 8.4 and 8.5 indicate that gearing limits were less important than high interest rates. Even so these answers exaggerate the effects of external monetary conditions because many of the companies which destocked to prevent an increase in gearing were reacting to self imposed limits, rather than externally imposed limits on borrowing. Also pressure on gearing flowed from the fall in demand as well as monetary conditions.

Gearing was important for some of the largest companies in the sample. One large company which had a heavy capital expenditure programme in progress, decided to clamp down on its gearing, and destocking was the main means of achieving this. Another large company with a new Chairman decided to substantially reduce its gearing. Decisions about the financing of British Leyland and British Steel were made after negotiations between the companies and the Government represented by the Department of Industry. Limits on gearing were not included as a cause of destocking for either company. For both companies the end year stocks to sales ratio had increased substantially since the early 1970's and there were other explanations for destocking. [19]

Companies impose their own, often conservative, gearing limits. At one retail company it was claimed that the sky was the limit for borrowing because of the company's property assets, but it did not gear up because financial analysts might make unfavourable comparisons of gearing with other retail companies. This company reduced its stocks to sales ratio in 1980, and slowed its expansion programme of opening new shops, to limit its borrowing. A manufacturer reduced gearing from nearly 40 per cent to 23 per cent between the beginning and end of its accounting year. The bank did not impose a limit on the company's borrowing, but there were conditions that the interest payments should not exceed a certain percentage of pre interest profits. If the company breached this condition the bank would want to charge assets, so the company set about reducing stocks to reduce borrowing to avoid a charge on its assets.

TAX RELIEF FOR STOCKBUILDING

Twenty out of forty one companies acknowledged that the change in tax rules for stock relief was a factor in destocking. Excess stocks had been held in the past to take advantage of the provisions described in Chapter 5, and in 1980 and 1981 stocks could be run down without liability to claw back.

Like slower inflation, tax relief for stocks affected changes in stocks in two main ways. Some companies deliberately brought forward purchases from the months following their accounting year end. Similarly some firms delayed deliveries at their year end to enlarge their stocks. [20] In addition, or alternatively, stock relief encouraged companies to allow stocks to increase, senior management did not start campaigns to reduce stocks because of the tax advantages of increases in stocks. This negative type of effect was difficult for companies to quantify. [21]

The possible reluctance of some companies to reveal that they had added to their stocks in order to reduce their tax liabilities has been described. The question was usually approached by asking whether stocks at the beginning of the latest accounting year were higher than they would have been in the absence of tax relief for stocks. Managers who claimed that their companies had not taken any advantage of stock relief were asked about other sources of deductions from taxable profits. Many of these companies had capital allowances or accumulated losses to set against taxable profits.

For eleven of the twenty companies for which the change in tax rules was a factor in destocking, it was possible to estimate the effects. An unweighted average showed 38 per cent of the reduction in the volume of stocks was attributable to tax rules. If a similar percentage applied to the other companies for which the changes in tax rules were reported to be a factor in destocking, and the change in these rules had no effect on other companies, then about 20 per cent of destocking by the whole sample was caused by the changes in tax rules for stocks. This estimate is based on an unweighted average. The largest manufacturing companies reckoned tax rules had not influenced their stockbuilding. For this reason the 20 per cent estimate exaggerates the effects of tax rules for destocking. Allowing for the largest companies not having taken advantage of stock relief, the 20 per cent figure should be reduced to perhaps 14 per cent.

It is estimated that about a quarter of the reduction in stocks caused by the change in tax rules is attributable to stocks 'held' only at the end of the financial year, but not throughout the year. Excluding these stocks, about ten per cent of the reduction in stocks was attributable to the run down of stocks acquired and held to obtain tax relief. Allowing for some under recording of the effects of tax changes, 12½ per cent of the decline in stocks may have been caused by changes to the tax rules.

EXCESS STOCKS

Earlier the implication of the fall in the stocks to sales ratio, that companies were over stocked was noted. Table 8.6 shows an analysis of the reasons for companies having held excess stocks; it is based on the explanations for destocking given by companies. The impact of tax provisions and inflation will be clear from the earlier discussion. The enquiry was made ex-post the destocking, and the fact that companies had been able to reduce stocks, indicated the existence of some slack which could be reduced.

Table 8.6 Excess Stocks

	Manufacturers		Retailers		Distributors	
	Yes	No	Yes	No	Yes	No
Company held excess stocks at the beginning of its accounting year	22	4	10	0	6	0
Reasons for holding excess stocks:						
tax provisions	12	10	5	5	3	3
inflation	11	11	3	7	5	1
slack	14	8	1	9	1	5
sales had increased more slowly than expected during the previous year	0	22	9	1	2	4

STEPS TAKEN TO REDUCE STOCKS

Companies can reduce stocks by cutting back purchases or increasing sales including exports. The main route to stock reductions was to cut back purchases, but some companies also sold off stock. Managers of the manufacturing companies in the sample were asked if they had increased exports to clear stocks. There were only two positive responses to this question. Two large companies had sold off stock in export markets to avoid spoiling the home market. Other companies had increased exports in part because of the fall in home demand, but it was not a case of selling off stocks, the companies planned to maintain their exports.

The synopses of the steps taken by firms to reduce stocks given in Appendix C illustrate the diverse steps taken by companies to economise on stocks.

CONCLUSIONS

The survey of the reasons for destocking showed the prime importance of the fall in demand for destocking. A second conclusion was that a combination of forces caused companies to destock; all the reasons or excuses for holding large stocks were knocked away during 1980 and 1981.

NOTES

[1] Most companies operate with annual budgets which include figures for stocks and sales and these budgets are subdivided on a monthly or quarterly basis. The ratio of stocks to sales in the past is normally taken as a guide to what the budgeted ratio should be. However, at the time of the enquiry the actual stocks to sales ratios for many companies had been distorted in recent years by inflation and the operation of tax relief related to stocks, and for a minority of companies by strikes or expected strikes and disruption of supplies.

[2] Officials of companies were asked whether they had planned to reduce stocks when they prepared their budgets for the accounting year in which they destocked. Seventeen out of 38 companies for which answers to this question were obtained had decided to destock when budgets were finalised (including four out of six retail companies).

[3] Four of the five giant manufacturing companies did not distinguish changes in work in progress in their published accounts. The 'weighted' fall in stocks is the fall in total stocks held by the companies. The unweighted fall is the average percentage fall in stocks as a percentage of sales between the beginning and the end of the accounting year.

[4] Changes in the volume of expected sales include changes caused by the acquisition or disposal of companies.

[5] In one extreme case demand for the products of a factory making motor components fell from a normal level of 70,000 units a week to 18,000 units at the worst point in the recession. The firm could not estimate the extent of the recovery and it based decisions including those involving redundancies on the actual level of activity. At the time of the visit a year later, production had recovered to 45,000 units and orders in hand required production of 60,000 units.

[6] In some cases firms changed the quality of products by, for example, changing the proportion of gold in jewellery.

[7] The budgeting process starts well before the beginning of an accounting year; subsidiaries of a large company may

prepare budgets four months before the start of the accounting year. Decisions affecting stock levels taken two months later may be based on different perceptions of the market outlook.

[8] A test was made of the exclusion of the least reliable estimates but their exclusion did not substantially reduce the percentage reduction in the overall unweighted average stocks to expected sales ratio.

[9] The qualifications relate to differences in the periods to which the estimates refer, changes in the composition of groups by disposal and acquisitions, and a tendency for the 1981/2 half year to include an extra week, increasing sales in the 1981/2 half year by about one and a half per cent compared to the previous year for the sample as a whole.

[10] Where companies rationalised their product ranges in response to the recession this was expected to reduce stocks. Where the reaction to the recession was to increase product ranges to get more business this was expected to increase stocks.

[11] Most firms write down some stocks at the end of each year. Firms were asked if there had been special or larger than usual write downs.

[12] Some retail companies did not attempt to anticipate price rises because of the difficulty of getting the merchandise right; the risk of piling up unsaleable goods was thought to be too great. For certain engineering companies which bought special types of steel, the order period was too long to take advantage of price increases. The elapse of time between placing an order and delivery was longer than between the announcement of an increase in price and it being implemented.

[13] One very large company allowed subsidiaries to increase stocks to deal with expected strikes (strikes in the Canadian nickel industry were given as the main example) but did not encourage subsidiaries to buy ahead of expected price increases.

[14] A retailer made suppliers finance a part of the peak Christmas stocks. One manufacturer delayed deliveries from suppliers from the end of a month to the beginning of the following month where this meant the company could take an extra month's credit.

[15] At one large company it was shown that closures were concentrated on factories with high stocks to sales ratios. The factories in trouble tended to pile up stocks because of difficulty in selling goods, and high stocks made operations unprofitable because of high interest charges. However, there was not a uniform tendency for

this relationship to apply. Closures were not always of stock intensive operations.

[16] For example, one manufacturer made calculations of whether it was worth continuing with some lines of business. For some of this company's lines, material costs represented between fifty and eighty per cent of the contract prices. Interest at 20 per cent could eliminate profits, but the company continued with the business because it would be difficult to win back orders when conditions improved. Another company made calculations when deciding order size but found that high rates of interest did not change decisions.

[17] Head offices usually added one or two per cent to market rates for overdrafts and deducted one or two per cent from market rates for deposits.

[18] Source Table 7.3. Manufacturing companies excluding the giants.

[19] If the Government did not force them to destock beyond a commercially prudent level by financial control, that would be in line with the Government's apparent policy of allowing these companies to operate commercially.

[20] In the absence of stock relief some companies would delay the receipt of goods at the year end to 'window dress' their balance sheets by reducing both stocks and creditors. At one company it was claimed that another reason for delaying inward deliveries at the year end had been to reduce the stock to be counted and to provide time for stock taking.

[21] An official of one company said about 20 per cent of his company's stocks at its 1979/80 year end were fictitious purchases in the sense that the company brought forward purchases, did not take delivery and the payment dates were not affected.

9 Evidence from companies which did not destock

The definition of 'not destocking' used for this chapter is companies which increased their stocks at recorded (historical cost) prices. As prices were rising this definition did not exclude some companies which reduced their stocks in volume terms. The chapter includes a comparison of the financial record of companies which did and did not destock, and records the results of discussions and correspondence with managers of a small sample of firms which did not destock.

THE FINANCIAL RECORD

The accounts of a sub-sample of firms which did not destock was analysed to pinpoint the salient characteristics of these companies. [1] Table 9.1 summarises the financial record of 17 manufacturing companies which did not destock and the sample of 21 manufacturing companies which did destock. Both sub-samples exclude giant companies. Plainly the average financial record of the companies which did not destock was a cut above that of companies which did so, in terms of growth of sales, trading profits, extraordinary items and cash flow. Their trading profits were a little higher in relation to sales in the base year and they did not fall. Interest payments were less in relation to sales and they rose very little.

A comparison not shown here of the financial record of the three giant manufacturing companies which increased their stocks with the five which destocked, showed a similar contrast, with the growth of sales faster, trading profits and cash flow from operations increasing not falling, extraordinary losses not increasing substantially and interest payments rising, but from a lower base in relation to sales. However, these contrasts did not apply to the record of two giant retail companies when compared to the record of the three giant retail companies which destocked. The financial records of the two groups were very similar. There were only four companies in the non giant retailer category which did not destock, so any conclusions based on comparisons with the seven non giant retail companies which destocked are tentative. For what they are worth the comparisons show a faster growth of sales and improved cash flow for the companies which did not destock, but a small fall in trading profits. On two out of three counts their trading performance was better than that of the non giant retail companies which destocked.

STOCKS TO SALES RATIO

Again for a very small sample of twelve companies which did not destock information about stock changes was obtained from companies. For eight of these companies stocks increased by an average of 14 per cent at current prices and four per cent in volume terms. The average expected increase in the volume of sales for these manufactures was 7½ per cent (compared to an expected fall of thirteen per cent for the companies which destocked) so the fall in the average stocks to expected sales ratio was two per cent (compared to ten per cent for the companies which destocked). However this rather stable average stock to expected sales ratio masked wide changes for the individual companies, from plus 16 per cent to minus 21 per cent.

REASONS FOR CHANGES IN STOCKS

None of the companies in the sample were under strong financial pressure at the beginning of the accounting year studied. It was not a case of these companies having high gearing but good trading conditions enabling them to over ride the financial squeeze. Nor was there evidence that these companies were attempting to destock but had been prevented from doing so.

Table 9.1

A Comparison of Financial Variables for Companies which Increased their Stocks by Value, and the Sample of Companies which Destocked (Manufacturing Companies excluding Giants)

	Samples of Companies which increased their stocks at recorded book value		Sample of Companies which destocked	
	1979/80	1980/81	1979/80	1980/81
		£m		
Number of companies	17		21	
World sales	1,562	1,702	2,007	1,941
UK Sales and Exports	1,259	1,361	1,567	1,496
UK Sales as % of world sales	81	80	78	77
Stocks at end of year	421	476	539	454
Stocks as % of world sales	27	28	27	23
Trading profit	133	133	141	90
Less Interest	-15	-16	-44	-55
	119	117	98	34
Less Taxation	-27	-31	-27	-15
Profit after Taxation	93	88	71	19
Extraordinary items	8	-5	-6	-30
Cash flow from operations	133	126	132	63

Two other possibilities were that the companies which did not destock had not increased stocks for tax reasons or as a hedge against inflation prior to 1980. In fact six out of nine companies had acquired limited extra stocks for tax purposes. Reversal of these 'tax' stocks had little impact because of their limited size. Similarly there was no evidence that slower inflation had much impact on the stock changes for these firms. Running down stocks held for these purposes may not have been so important for companies which did not destock as for the sample of firms which destocked. These results, especially the one for tax changes are important, though very tentative, because of the small size of the sample.

It is more difficult for managers to explain why they did not reduce stocks than why they did. However some characteristics of the sample contributing to increased stocks (at recorded prices) were that four out of twelve of the companies had taken over companies and that five had had very rapid expansion of sales. Special factors also contributed: one company was developing a new line for which the stocks to sales ratio was high; one had recently raised finance by a rights issue; one had expanded stocks overseas as a result of opening new stores; one distributed fuel, and mild weather towards the end of its accounting year left the company with large year end stocks; one company had entered into contracts to import machine tools and these piled up in stock when demand slumped; for one company, a subsidiary of a giant, a switch in sales from small batch work to much larger batches for export had resulted in some loss of stock control, and for one retailer the Christmas trade was less buoyant than expected and extra stock was left over.

NOTES

[1] Accounts were obtained from 94 companies which did not destock. Accounts for a sub-sample of 31 companies were analysed: 20 manufacturers including three giants, six retail companies including two giants, and five distributors.

10 The causes of destocking

It is not possible to squeeze a complete picture of the causes of destocking from the evidence assembled. The forces which contributed to the destocking are known, but the relative importance of some of the forces is uncertain.

THE SAMPLES

Table 10.1 shows the changes in volume of stocks for the 240 companies which provided copies of their published accounts and which were not excluded because of the industry or size restrictions. [1] These companies held about thirty per cent of stocks held in manufacturing industries at the end of 1979 and 22 per cent of retail stocks. The samples of companies from which information was obtained for the enquiry held about 13 per cent of manufacturing and 12 per cent of retail stocks.

One division of companies shown in Table 10.1 is between companies which increased stocks at recorded book values, and the companies which destocked in terms of recorded book values. The first group increased the volume of their stocks by four per cent. [2] Stocks held by the second group of companies fell by nearly 17 per cent. The changes in stocks of these two groups of companies is closely matched by the changes in stocks of the two samples of companies which were studied.

Table 10.1
Changes in Stocks

	Number of Companies	Stocks at the end of: 1979/80 £m	1980/81 £m	Cost of Sales Adjustment £m	Change in Stocks £m	%
COMPANIES FOR WHICH ACCOUNTS WERE RECEIVED						
Companies which increased their stocks at recorded book prices:						
Manufacturers	65	3,233	3,642	255	+154	+ 4.4
Retailers	16	481	529	40	+8	+ 1.5
Distributors	13	189	221	19	+13	+ 6.2
Total	94	3,903	4,392	314	+175	+ 4.1
Companies which destocked:						
Manufacturers	107	8,395	7,474	553	-1,474	-16.5
Retailers	19	1,126	1,020	76	-182	-15.1
Distributors	20	1,068	939	126	-255	-21.4
Total	146	10,589	9,433	755	-1,911	-16.8
All Companies:						
Manufacturers	172	11,628	11,116	808	-1,320	-10.6
Retailers	35	1,607	1,549	116	-174	-10.1
Distributors	33	1,257	1,160	145	-242	-17.3
Total	240	14,492	13,825	1,069	-1,736	-11.2
SAMPLES OF COMPANIES STUDIED						
Companies which increased their stocks at recorded book prices:						
Manufacturers	4	880	992	60	+52	+5.5
Retailers	3	182	198	14	+2	+1.0
Disbributors	1	43	63	3	+17	+37.0
Total	8	1,105	1,253	77	+71	+6.0
Companies which destocked:						
Manufacturers	26	4,824	4,255	320	-889	-17.3
Retailers	10	856	771	62	-147	-16.0
Distributors	6	690	627	103	-166	-20.9
Total	42	6,370	5,653	485	-1,202	-17.5
All Companies in the samples:						
Manufacturers	30	5,704	5,247	380	-837	-13.8
Retailers	13	1,038	969	76	-145	-13.0
Distributors	7	733	690	106	-149	-17.8
Total	50	7,475	6,906	562	-1,131	-14.1

A comparison of the distribution of stock changes for companies operating in manufacturing industries for which published accounts were received and the main sample of companies which destocked is shown in Diagram 10.1. Here the matching of population and sample is less close. The sample is drawn disporportionately from the group of companies which reduced their stocks by 15 to 20 per cent. Inevitably there are qualifications to conclusions based on information drawn from small samples. Nevertheless the samples are the best available and they are used to assess the causes of destocking.

CONFLICTS OF EVIDENCE

So far the micro and macro level evidence has been described separately. In this section a conflict of evidence is considered.

Attention has been focused on the ratio of stocks to sales and production. Micro and macro estimates of changes in the components of these ratios and the ratios are shown in Table 10.2. The sample of manufacturing companies which destocked reduced their stocks more sharply than manufacturing industry as a whole, reflecting the method of selecting the sample. The reduction in their expected sales, 13 per cent, was in line with the fall in actual production for the whole of manufacturing industry, 14.2 per cent. However as the sample were destocking their production was falling faster than their sales. Changes in their work in progress provide a clue to changes in their rates of production. The weighted reduction in work in progress of 15 per cent (and 18 per cent unweighted) by the sample of manufacturers (excluding the giants) at recorded book prices, suggests that when adjusted for price increases, work in progress fell by about 25 (and 29) per cent. [3] If changes in work in progress indicate the extent of changes in production, then production fell more than expected sales. A part of the differences between movements of the micro stocks to sales, and the macro stocks to production, ratios was caused by the differing movement of expected sales and production for the sample of manufacturing companies which destocked. For both manufacturing and retailing some difference would be expected because the sample of companies which destocked was selected because of their destocking.

Diagram 10.1

Distribution of Companies by Percentage Change in the Volume of Stocks

(Manufacturing Companies including the Giants)

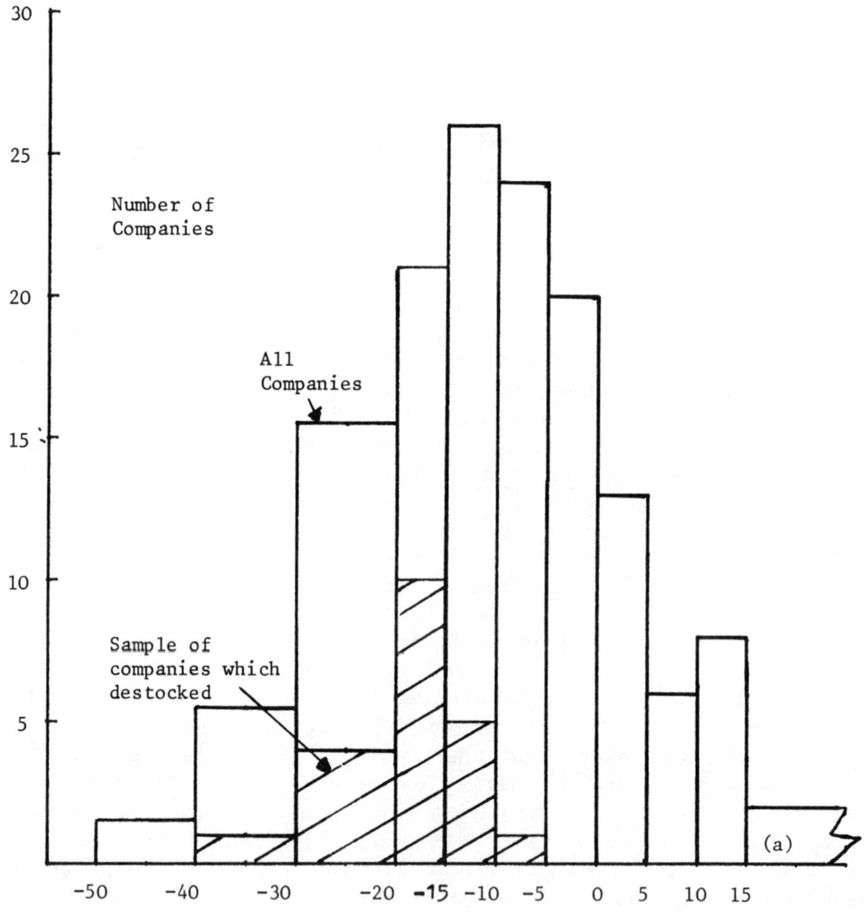

(a) Average for 9 observations 43.4

Table 10.2
The Ratio of Stocks to Sales and Production

	Micro estimates.[a] Sample of firms which destocked. Data for their accounting years		Macro estimates.[b] Whole Industry (1st Q 1980 to 1st Q 1981)
	Weighted	Unweighted	
	Percentage change		
Manufacturing			
1. Volume of stocks	-19	-24	-8.0
2. Expected sales volume	-13	-13	
Production			-14.2
3. Ratio of:			
Stocks to expected sales	-7	-12	
Stocks to production			+7.2 (4th Q 1979 to 4th Q 1980)
Retailing			
4. Volume of stocks	-15	-16	-5.7
5. Expected sales volume	-4	-4	
Actual sales volume			-0.9
6. Ratio of:			
Stocks to expected sales	-11	-13	
Stocks to sales			-4.8

a For the micro ratio, expected sales are for the quarter following that to which the stocks data relate. For the macro estimates, stocks are related to production during the quarter preceding the date.

b The period was selected to coincide with the average accounting year ends for sample companies.

Source for macro statistics: ETAS 1984.

EXPECTATIONS

The potential importance of changes in expectations was described in Chapter 4. Managers' expectations for sales slumped in 1980 as described in Chapter 8. For many manufacturers there were good reasons for this change in expectations. In the event the sales of certain retailers fell less than they expected; in retrospect their reactions to the recession were exaggerated. In any case retailers reversed their destocking in 1981. In 1980 expectations deteriorated, and managers acted on the new expectations. They did not assume the economy would rapidly adjust to restore a high level of demand, and act upon that assumption.

SUMMING UP

Assumptions are required to assess the causes of destocking from the evidence available. The initial assumptions made are that:

1. The population of companies is made up of two groups; companies which destocked and companies which did not change their stocks at all.
2. An explanation for destocking by the group of companies which destocked then explains the overall destocking.
3. The main sample of 42 companies which destocked fairly represents the population of companies which destocked.

Starting with this set of assumptions, the evidence about destocking obtained from the main sample and described in Chapter 8 is used to account for destocking. Even so, it is not possible to allot to each cause of destocking a precise portion of the destocking, principally because managers do not make decisions in response to single events but to a whole set of circumstances.

The prime direct cause of destocking by companies was the reduction in demand not the financial squeeze. The reduction in sales led to a fall in stocks through the stocks to sales relationship, and was reinforced by the effects of the fall in demand on profits and cash flow. The financial squeeze, operating through high interest rates, was the second factor and the third one was the change in the treatment of stockbuilding for tax purposes. The relative scores out of ten for the pressures on firms to destock may have been: the fall in demand, six, the financial squeeze, two, tax changes, one and a quarter, other causes including the slow down in inflation, three quarters. These estimates are no more than best guesses based on the evidence collected from companies which destocked.

The basis for the estimates starts with the effects of tax changes given in Chapter 8. Destocking caused by changes in the tax rules accounted for perhaps $12\frac{1}{2}$ per cent of the destocking. The monetary squeeze operating through high interest rates was of similar importance to tax relief according to the responses in Table 8.4, though somewhat less important when the main factors causing destocking were considered (Table 8.5). However high interest rates reduced profits and cash flow as well as directly triggering destocking. Plainly the decline in demand was the main direct impulse for destocking so it gets the highest score.

The effects of relaxing the assumptions are now considered. If in fact destocking was the result of some firms not increasing their stocks as much as they otherwise would have done, and others reducing their stocks more than they would have done - a more plausible set of assumptions - the reasons for firms not increasing their stocks enter the assessment. These firms are represented by the first category of companies shown in Table 10.1. They held less than one third of the stocks held by the companies whose accounts were analysed for this table. The comparisons in Chapter 9 which relate to a sample of these companies suggest that the financial squeeze and the changes in tax rules were less important for these companies than for companies which destocked. (In Table 9.1 the companies which did not destock are shown to have paid less interest and for the very small sample for which information was obtained from managers, the change in tax rules was less important). Relaxation of the initial assumptions could therefore increase the relative importance of the decline in demand as the other factors may have been less important for firms which did not destock, but we cannot be sure of this.

The main caveat to transferring the conclusions based on micro level evidence to a macro level is that the reduction in stocks was a component of the reduction in demand. In Chapter 3 it was shown that compared to the <u>no change</u> alternative position, the decline in stocks was an important component of the reduction in demand during 1980, so the reduction in stocks including destocking attributable to the financial squeeze and changes in the tax treatment of stocks reduced demand and this led to a further fall in stocks. In this scenario major causes of destocking could be those independent of demand - the financial squeeze and the change in the tax treatment of stocks. In addition to their direct effect in reducing stocks, by reducing demand for goods for stockbuilding, they led to further destocking.

The destocking caused by the decline in demand for stockbuilding has to be recycled to its components. The analysis in Chapter 3 suggests that compared to the no change alternative, very approximately half of the decline in demand during the year from the second quarter of 1980 to the first quarter of 1981 was attributable to destocking (Diagram 3.3). For reasons given in Chapter 3 these estimates are not precise. Nonetheless it is clear that a substantial part of the score for demand should be recycled. In the event half the score for demand was transferred to give the final scores out of ten of four and three quarters for demand, two and a half for the financial squeeze, one and three quarters for changes in tax rules and one for other factors. These estimates refer to destocking compared to the no change alternative position. When a comparison is made with a growing economy, destocking and the reasons for destocking were much less important factors in the recession, for the reasons described in Chapter 3.

NOTES

[1] The reasons for excluding some companies are described in Appendix A.

[2] The change in stocks includes stocks acquired by take overs.

[3] The change in the national income deflator for work in progress between the end of 1979 and the end of 1980 was used to adjust current values.

11 Summary and conclusions

THE IMPORTANCE OF DESTOCKING IN THE RECESSION

1. The apparent importance of destocking in the recession depends upon the assumptions made about the hypothetical growth of the economy in the absence of the recession. When the shortfall of demand relative to growth of aggregate demand required for three per cent growth of GDP (the rate of growth required to stabilise unemployment) is used as a basis for comparison, destocking contributed about a fifth of the demand deficiency in 1980, but accounted for only five per cent of the shortfall of demand by the fourth quarter of 1981. (Diagram 3.2).

2. Compared to the no change alternative position, with no growth of GDP from the beginning of the recession, destocking accounted for about half of the decline in GDP during 1980 and the first half of 1981 (Diagram 3.3). For manufacturing industries destocking averaged about half of the decline in output in the second half of 1980, one third during the first half of 1981, but only ten per cent during the second half of 1981 (Diagram 3.4). The importance of destocking during the recession was exaggerated because comparisons were made with the misleading no change alternative.

THE SURVEY OF COMPANIES WHICH DESTOCKED

3. Information about the reasons for destocking was obtained from 42 companies which destocked. The companies approached were selected from companies which reduced their stocks in volume terms. The response rate from all the companies approached was 51 per cent, but was much higher for retail companies. Destocking by the sample of 42 companies represented about a quarter of the estimated destocking in the UK in 1980.

THE RATIO OF STOCKS TO OUTPUT AND SALES DURING THE 1970's

4. During the 1970's the ratios of stocks to output for manufacturing industries and stocks to sales for retailing, increased above the extrapolated trends estimated from data for the period 1959 to 1971. (Diagrams 6.3 to 6.7).

5. Changes in the composition of the output of manufacturing industry at the industry group level did not account for the change in the stocks to output ratio for manufacturing during the 1970's. (Chapter 6).

6. The increase in stocks to output and sales ratios occurred simultaneously with an acceleration in the rate of inflation and related changes in the tax treatment of stocks which are described in Chapter 5. The treatment of stockbuilding for corporation tax purposes gave many companies an incentive to increase the volume of their stocks at the end of each accounting year from 1975 until 1980.

7. About half the sample of companies which destocked had taken some advantage of the tax relief for increases in the volume of stocks. This had been accomplished by bringing forward purchases at the end of companies' accounting years and by allowing stocks to build up. Many of the companies which did not take advantage of the rules had losses or capital allowances to set against profits for tax purposes. Fewer companies increased stocks to take advantage of inflation. (Chapter 8).

8. The study provides insights into the effects of inflation. The micro evidence suggests that increases in the stocks to output and sales ratios from 1975 were in part caused by inflation and the form of stock relief which was adopted. Accumulation of the excess stocks buoyed up demand and output of the economy for a while in the 1970's, but destocking at

some time was inevitable if inflation was to be reduced and the tax rules put on a sound basis.

9. The reduction in stocks by the sample of companies which destocked was greater than the fall in their expected sales, and their stocks to expected sales ratio fell.

REASONS FOR DESTOCKING

10. A well substantiated, though unsurprising, result of the enquiry was to find that there were many pressures on companies to destock, managers reacted to a combination of pressures by reducing stocks.

11. Both the reduction in demand and high interest rates reduced the cash flow of companies. This operated as a semi automatic pressure for destocking. Within many companies monitoring of cash flow is an important control on operating businesses, and a reduction of stocks is the most readily available source of an improvement in cash flow. Operating businesses reduced stocks to offset the reduction in cash flow and/or to meet cash flow targets. (Chapter 8).

12. Very few companies acknowledged that they made direct use of the rate of interest to decide the level of stocks to hold. Also forty per cent of the manufacturing companies did not charge their operating businesses interest. High interest rates cause destocking by reducing profits and cash flow and by providing an attractive return on funds released from stockholding. (Chapter 8).

13. Externally imposed gearing and borrowing restrictions were not important for most of the companies in the sample. However, internally set gearing limits, or cash flow targets, were important, especially for some of the largest companies in the sample of companies which destocked. (Chapter 8).

14. One objective of the enquiry was to establish the relative importance of demand changes and the financial squeeze as causes of destocking. In Chapter 7 it was shown that the impact of high interest rates on the profits of the sample of companies which destocked was less than the decline in trading profits. Managers' answers to questions about the factors causing destocking described in Chapter 8 also showed the prime importance of the decline in demand, including destocking, for causing destocking by manufacturing companies. The financial

squeeze was secondary. Some retail companies which were less affected by the reduction in demand, reduced their stocks in response to high interest rates they could earn in financial markets.

SUMMARY OF ESTIMATES

15. Tentative estimates of the direct contribution of the pressures on firms to destock were presented in Chapter 10. On the basis of assumptions described in that chapter the following scores out of ten were allotted:- the fall in demand, six, the financial squeeze, two, tax changes one and a quarter, other causes, three quarters. When the effects of destocking on demand were reallocated to the other causes of destocking, the scores were the fall in demand, four and three quarters, the financial squeeze two and a half, tax changes, one and three quarters, other forces, one.

Appendix A
The enquiry

THE ENQUIRY

The first step in selecting companies to approach for the enquiry was to ask companies whose accounts were analysed in the Investors Chronicle to provide a copy of their accounts [1]. Companies whose main activities were outside the manufacturing, retailing and distribution sectors, and companies with a turnover of less than £20m were excluded.

Accounts were obtained for more than three hundred companies with accounting year ends from July 31st 1980 to August 31st 1981. Companies which had substantially reduced their stock in volume terms (in most cases by more than ten per cent) and whose head offices were not too far distant from Cambridge were then selected [2]. The regional selection of companies was imposed to limit the cost of the project. Although it introduced a regional bias, many companies whose head office is in the South East operate factories in other regions. Soon after the start of the project it was decided to exclude food manufacture, and the tobacco and brewing industries.

In most cases a letter was sent to the Chairman or Managing Director of each company selected, asking for an opportunity to discuss the change in his company's stocks, the company's stocks to sales ratio and the reasons for changes in stocks. Forty-two of the eighty-two companies approached arranged an interview or provided information by letter and telephone [3]. In addition six companies provided some information about changes in their stocks but not sufficient data to be included in the analyses. The response rate from retail companies, more than eighty per cent, contrasted with 46 per cent for manufacturing companies.

The financial record of manufacturing companies which destocked and provided information for the study and the manufacturing companies approached which did not provide this information is compared in Tables A.1 and A.2. In relation to sales, the aggregate profits and cash flow of the sample of companies which collaborated were a little lower, and fell more than those of the companies which did not provide information for the study (Table A.1). The unweighted declines in trading profits, interest, profits before tax and cash flow as a percentage of sales in 1980/81 were all greater for the companies which did not collaborate (Table A.2) [4]. However the differences do not seem of sufficient magnitude to distort the conclusions based on information collected from companies which collaborated.

The industrial mix of the twenty-six manufacturing companies which provided information for the study was: food, one; chemicals and allied trades, four; steel and metal goods, two; engineering and allied trades, seven; textiles, three; clothes and leather goods, two; furniture, three; and other manufacturing, four. Four of the ten retailing companies were mail order houses. Two of the distributors dealt in electronic components, one in oil, one in motor vehicles, one in ships stores and tackle and one in engineering products.

It was left to each company to nominate the official who would discuss changes in stocks. Most of the discussions were with the finance director or a member of his staff or the planning staff. For nine companies the chief executive dealt with the enquiry. For four companies the discussions were with managers of subsidiary companies, not the group headquarters.

An analysis of the companies whose accounts were received is shown in Table A.3. One hundred and one companies were excluded because of the size and industry restrictions. Of the remaining companies 146, sixty-one per cent, destocked and 94, thirty-nine per cent, increased their stocks at recorded book prices.

Table A.1

A Comparison of the Accounting Records of Companies which Destocked (Manufacturing companies excluding the giants)

	Sample of companies which destocked		Companies which did not provide detailed information for the enquiry	
Number of companies	21		30	
	1979/80 £m	1980/81 £m	1979/80 £m	1980/81 £m
World sales	2,007	1,941	2,636	2,613
U.K. sales plus exports	1,567	1,496		1,982
(U.K. sales and exports as % of world sales)	78.1	77.1		75.9
Stocks at the end of the year	539	454	682	594
(Stocks as % of world sales)	26.9	23.4	25.9	22.7
Trading profit	141	90	201	140
less interest	-44	-55	-38	-49
Profit before tax	97	35	163	91
Cash flow from operations	132	63	179	111

Table A.2

A Comparison of Profits, Interest and Cash Flow as a Percentage of Sales in 1980/81 for Companies which Destocked
(Manufacturing companies, including the giants)

	Samples of companies which destocked		Companies which did not provide detailed information for the enquiry	
Number of companies	26		31	
	(unweighted averages)			
	1979/80	1980/81	1979/80	1980/81
Trading profits	5.9	3.1	6.4	3.0
Interest	-1.9	-2.2	-1.8	-2.3
Profit before tax	4.0	0.9	4.6	0.7
Cash flow	5.7	1.8	7.0	1.4

Table A.3
Company Accounts Received

Total		341
Companies which destocked:		
Companies approached	82	
Companies which reduced their stocks but whose head office was too far distant from Cambridge	28	
Other companies which destocked but which were not approached [a]	36	146
Companies which increased their stocks at recorded book prices		94
Other Companies:		
Food, confectionary, brewing and tobacco companies	29	
International companies [b]	6	
Companies whose main operations were outside manufacturing, retailing and distribution sectors	16	
Companies with sales of less than £20 million	50	101

[a] These companies were not approached because of the limited resources available for the study. No systematic selection procedure was used to select which of the companies which destocked to approach (apart from the regional restriction).

[b] Companies whose overseas operations accounted for more than fifty per cent of sales.

NOTES

[1] Analysis of the accounts by the Investors Chronicle signalled the accounts had been published.
[2] Companies whose head office was in Scotland, Wales, the West and Northern England were excluded. Some companies in the Midlands, the North West and Yorkshire were included to provide a representative coverage of manufacturing apart from food manufacture and brewing.
[3] The author visited thirty-five of the companies.
[4] The average decline in sales was also greater for the companies which did not co-operate 3.6 compared to 2.4 per cent.

Appendix B
Check list of questions for interviews

CHECK LIST OF QUESTIONS FOR INTERVIEWS

Each interview started with a review of the changes in the company's stocks. Most discussions developed with the official of the company explaining the reasons for his company destocking. This description was supplemented by answers to the following questions.

1. Can you explain why stocks were reduced during the 1980/81 accounting year?
2. Can you divide the change in stocks into changes stemming from:
   (a) a fall in demand?
   If possible obtain the stocks/expected sales ratio at the end of the last two accounting years
   (b) the financial squeeze?
   (c) other factors?
3. Were stocks in balance at the beginning of the period?
4. What were the effects on stocks of:
   (a) closures?
   (b) rationalisation of the product range or components?
   (c) extension of the product range?
5. What were the effects on stocks of the financial squeeze?
   Did the financial squeeze operate through:
   (a) increases in interest rates?
   (b) a profits squeeze and/or cash flow squeeze?
   What caused them?
   (c) the availability of loans?
   Does your company have any rules for its gearing?
6. Have changes in the expected rate of inflation affected stocks?
7. What effects do high rates of interest have?
   Are interest rates charged to subsidiaries?
8. Were changes in the availability of supplies a factor affecting stocks?
9. Were there any special write downs of stocks?

10. How, if at all, did the changes in tax rules for relief on stocks influence stocks and changes in stocks?
11. Were there any other causes of the reduction of stocks?
12. Was the reduction in stocks planned?
    Have stocks changed in line with plans in earlier years?
13. Are further changes in stocks planned?
14. Were stocks the only or main item to be squeezed?
15. Were falling stocks a prelude to falling exports and/or investment?
16. How does the head office control stocks?
    Were there any changes in methods in 1980?
17. Were there any effects of the recession on the influence of different groups of managers?
18. What were the three most important factors causing the reduction in stocks?

Appendix C
Reasons for destocking and steps taken to reduce stocks

The purpose of this Appendix is to provide another guide to the factors which managers of companies thought important for decisions to destock and to illustrate the measures they took to reduce stocks. Reference to changes in sales refer to volume changes unless sales in money terms (at current prices) are referred to in the text. The information given for each company is limited in order to maintain the anonymity of companies.

MANUFACTURERS

1. The company reduced its UK stocks by about 20 per cent during 1980. There was a substantial reduction in expected sales for the first quarter of 1981 compared to the first quarter of 1980, and the fall in the stock to sales ratio was about five per cent. After a buoyant second half of 1979, many subsidiaries had a bad second quarter in 1980 and confidence ebbed. The reduction in sales was mainly of sales to the home market. The high sterling exchange rate made continental firms very competitive in the UK market and squeezed profits. The company was not affected by the financial squeeze.

The reduction in stocks was not brought about by directives from the head office, but there were discussions about stocks -

ideas about destocking went around the group. The company had an effective stock control system based on control of volumes. In effect volume limits were set for subsidiaries' stocks and these limits could only be changed by the parent company which reviewed the limits periodically.

2. The company reduced its stocks by 15 per cent during 1980. At the end of 1979 the company's forecasts showed an increase in stocks during 1980. In the first quarter of 1980 all went well, sales and profits rose, but so did stocks. In April 1980, business in the UK fell dramatically and between the first and third quarters of 1980 external sales from the UK operations fell by twenty per cent. Later in the year the fall in demand spread to other parts of Europe.

The company operated within a self imposed gearing ratio of between 30 and 40 per cent of equity funds. Faced with the fall in sales, profits and cash flow and a heavy capital expenditure programme which it would not be wise to cut, the need to increase cash flow focused on stocks. Divisions of the company were directed to cut stocks by, for example, selling off stocks of sub-standard products.

3. The company reduced stocks by 18 per cent. The reduction was not a direct result of the recession or financial squeeze. The cause of the destocking was that the company was over-stocked at the beginning of the year. Stocks had risen and no one had done anything about it. When it was pointed out that they could earn 15 per cent on the proceeds of destocking, the counter argument had been that they would lose 52 per cent in tax. Rapid inflation had been another factor justifying high levels of stocks. The fall in demand at home had squeezed profits though the fall in sales to the home market had been made up by increased exports. The profits squeeze meant they had to increase efficiency - hence the destocking.

The destocking was achieved by setting targets for the operating companies. The sales and stocks budgets prepared by operating companies were scaled down at the head office. A director visited operating units, inspected all stocks and checked on slow moving items.

4. The company reduced stocks by 27 per cent. The decline in demand and the increase in interest rates resulted in a financial crisis for the company. By the end of 1980 the gearing ratio exceeded 1 to 1. In the past stock control had not been close. During 1980 the management of the business came to be focused on cash flow. Stocks were reduced from the equivalent of 36 weeks expected sales at the beginning of the

year to 23 weeks at the end of the year.

5. The company reduced stocks by 15 per cent. The reduction in stocks was a deliberate response to an expected fall in demand from distributors who would destock, not final consumers. The company did have higher 'book' stocks because of the tax rules. It was not a case of having more physical stock in the factories but of more paper entries. Goods were booked in early. The financial squeeze and higher interest rates had no effect. Nor did slower inflation; the company did not speculate on price rises by acquiring additional stocks.

The company up-dated its plans each month. In February and March 1980 the management did not foresee the reduction in demand. The main planning period for the company was April and May when there had been time to assimilate the Budget. In May 1980 a reduction in demand was foreseen and it was decided to reduce stocks. In December 1980 deliveries at one factory were stopped for three weeks to reduce stocks.

6. The company reduced its stocks by 19 per cent. The main factors causing the reduction were a fall in demand, the financial squeeze and the effects of a strike. At the beginning of the year the company held excess stocks of raw materials which had built up during a strike which lasted through the final quarter of 1979/80. The first quarter of 1980/81 was buoyant as sales delayed by the strike were completed, then business slumped. During the strike debtors paid accounts and expenditure was reduced, but when the company started up again there was a cash outflow for wages and materials and no inflow. The financial squeeze operated through cash limits, not high interest rates. In turn the company controlled its subsidiaries through cash budgets.

7. Since 1977 the management had realised that there were serious problems at the company's largest division, but not much was done until 1979. From 1979 cash flow was very tight. Sales were twenty per cent below budget in 1980 and profitability took a hammering because of the high exchange rate which made it difficult to pass on costs in the home market and shrank profit margins on exports. Tough decisions were taken to return the division to profitability by closures, redundancy and the introduction of new products.

The head office set targets for cash flow for subsidiaries and demanded a reduction in stocks as this was the main area of flexibility. Strike insurance stocks were cut. Production control was improved so as to reduce rejects and the products awaiting repair, and there were lay offs to drive down stocks of finished goods.

Reductions in stocks were planned for 1978 and 1979 but did not occur. In 1980 and 1981 managers took the decisions required to reduce stocks.

8. The company reduced stocks by 22 per cent. A decline in sales was the main cause of the fall in stocks. Expected sales at the end of the year were about a quarter below those at the end of the previous year. The decline in demand from the motor manufacturers the company supplied was very sharp partly because the company had lost markets for a product for which it had had a monopoly. Customer companies had cut purchases more than their own sales, they reduced their own stocks, switched purchases to European suppliers and redesigned some products in a way that cut out the company's product. The decline in profitability had a shock effect; previously the company had had an unbroken record of rapidly rising profits. The financial squeeze did not have much impact on destocking.

At June 1980, stocks were twice the level the managers would like. Ideally stocks should be about twelve weeks sales (at cost of sales prices). Apart from the tax advantages another factor causing the company to have excess stocks was stocks acquired through acquisitions of companies. A factor which made it difficult to reduce stocks of finished goods was the need to maintain employment.

9. Stocks were reduced by 18 per cent and the stocks to expected sales ratio fell by 12 per cent. One reason for the decline in the stocks to sales ratio was a profit squeeze. There had been a build up of stocks prior to 1980. The group had been cash rich and though it had made no deliberate attempts to get tax relief by holding extra stocks, tax relief could have been a factor justifying the slack. Similarly rapid inflation may have justified high stocks. It had become harder to earn profits in 1980 and so controls on stocks had been increased. Also four factories had been closed.

10. The company reduced its stocks by 17 per cent. The primary explanation for the reduction in stocks was the change in tax provisions to remove claw back. The first quarter of 1980 was buoyant because customers bought to protect themselves against possible shortages caused by the steel strike. The second quarter of 1980 was very bad and the head office put pressure on operating companies to reduce stocks. Stocks had been allowed to build up for tax purposes and the decision to destock was a reflex to the perceived removal of the need to

hold stocks for tax purposes. Also profits were down and materials were in easy supply. The company had cash to invest and was not affected by the financial squeeze. The company bought some expensive materials on an opportunistic basis, but prices were not expected to rise at the end of the year so the company did not buy ahead.

11. For the year 1979/80 the company budgeted for a 16 per cent increase in the value of stocks. In the event stocks were reduced by 16 per cent in real terms. Trade was buoyant until March 1980 when there was a drastic fall in home sales which were not affected by imports. One factor in the reduction in stocks was the introduction of a cash control system in 1979 which included charging subsidiaries interest on working capital. Easier availability of supplies was another factor contributing to destocking.

12. Stocks shown in the balance sheet fell by 18 per cent in money terms. At the beginning of 1980, twenty per cent of stocks were held by suppliers and were in the books for tax purposes. These stocks were reduced by a quarter during the year and other stocks by 15 per cent, while sales early in 1981 were twenty per cent above those early in 1980. The reasons for the reduction in stocks were the sale of a subsidiary and closure of four factories in a part of the business where stock turnover was lowest. Also management took action to improve efficiency by reducing stocks. The company had not been much affected by the recession - import competition was slight and the reaction of the management had been to go out and sell more in the home market. The financial squeeze had not operated on them.

13. The company manufactured clothes for a multiple retailer, other retailers and for sale through its own shops. The company reduced stocks by 27 per cent. It had got into serious trouble in 1980. Projections indicated that the company's overdraft would rise to twice shareholders' funds (on the basis of unchanged policies). Apart from the effects of the high interest rates the company had been adversely affected by fashion changes. The trigger for the reduction in stocks was this cash crisis. There was slack in stocks to cut into; the rate of stock turnover for the retailing division was less than twice a year.

The company cut stocks by starting manufacture of winter coats a month later. The retailing division reduced the number of shops from 220 to 160 and adopted a policy of buying what was being demanded rather than what the manufacturing division produced, where necessary by increasing its purchases from outside the group. The head office had set targets for reductions in stocks by subsidiaries.

14. During the 1970's the company had allowed stocks to build up. There had been a waiting list for the companys' products and the aim had been to speed up deliveries. The tax advantages of increasing stocks may have played an unconscious part in this build up. Between the early 1970's and 1979, the ratio of annual turnover to stock fell from five to three and a third.

During the year to July 1981 the company reduced its stocks by 19 per cent. Stocks were pared because of a reduction in demand - once retailers realised supplies were more readily available they had cut back their own stocks. Also the management wanted to hold down borrowing. The Chairman aimed to keep borrowing to one-third of net assets. Managers were made aware that a reduction in stocks was required and reacted to this. The management intended to get the rate of stock turnover up to five times in 1984.

15. In March 1980 the company's gearing ratio (borrowing as a percentage of equity funds) reached 70 per cent. The company made a policy decision to reduce gearing. High interest rates and the reduction in demand contributed to the decision. Stocks were reduced by more than 25 per cent and the stocks to expected sales ratio by 22 per cent. This was achieved by rationalisation - selling off businesses and closing lines - operating with smaller stocks and rationalising the distribution network.

16. For its continuing UK businesses, the company reduced its stocks by 41 per cent. A 25 per cent reduction was attributable to the run down of an earlier build up of stocks to gain tax relief. The second factor was a policy decision to stay liquid, and the third factor was a decline in demand

The directors of the company had used the 1975 stocks to sales ratios as the basis for target stock reductions for subsidiaries. The targets set implied lower stocks to sales ratios than those achieved in 1975. The subsidiaries were given a list of 'good housekeeping' practices for reducing their stocks and to take advantage of destocking by other firms to get price reductions.

17. The company reduced its stocks by a quarter and its stocks to sales ratio by 11 per cent. Early in the company's financial year revised budgets indicated that the company's gearing ratio would rise to 70 per cent. Subsidiaries were

given targets for increasing their cash flow. The directors of the holding company decided not to provide finance which would be borrowed at high rates of interest for subsidiaries whose current and expected rates of profit were much lower than the rate of interest.

18. The company reduced its stocks by 26 per cent. The volume of expected sales fell by between ten and fifteen per cent indicating a fall in the stocks to sales ratio. The causes of destocking were the fall in activity and the priority the company gave to improving cash flow. From the autumn of 1979, the number and size of orders from retailers declined. Retailers started ordering on a hand-to-mouth basis. The high exchange rate was a factor causing recession, but there was also a lack of confidence.

The priority given to improving cash flow was associated with the appointment of a new Chairman. The divisions were set cash flow targets. The basis for these targets was not very scientific - they were related to total capital employed. The divisions were left to meet the targets at a time of recession. The company and the divisions took a fresh look at businesses and decided which ones they wanted to retain; they could not carry unprofitable businesses through the recession. The operating units with high stocks were self selecting for closure and cut backs. Disproportionately high stocks were associated with falling sales and low profits.

19. The company reduced its UK stocks by nearly thirty per cent. The pressures for reducing stocks were the decline in business and a decision to reduce gearing because of the high interest rates and low profits. Stocks of businesses which were closed accounted for about sixty per cent of the decline in stocks.

20. The company reduced stocks by 29 per cent. The main reason for the decline was a policy of conserving cash. The company did not wish the bank to create a charge on its assets. At the beginning of the year its gearing ratio was 35 per cent, but there were agreements with the bank about the interest cover (the ratio of interest payments to pre-interest profits) which were in danger of being breached because of high interest rates and squeezed profits, so the company aimed to reduce its borrowing. Also the management wanted to build up cash to take advantage of any favourable opportunities for takeovers. Other factors causing destocking were the decline in demand, the sale of some businesses and to avoid the risks of holding large stocks.

The run-down of stocks was achieved by getting subsidiaries to stick to budgets which were set to reduce stocks, particularly the stocks of loss making companies.

RETAILERS

21. The company reduced its stocks by more than 15 per cent. The volume of expected and actual sales for the first quarter of 1981 were about the same as for 1980 so the decline in stocks reflected a fall in the stocks to expected sales ratio.

The main reasons for the reduction in stocks were the change in the tax rules. At the beginning of 1980 the company held some excess stocks because of the tax advantages for holding stocks. Purchases had been brought forward towards the end of the previous year and some slack had built up. High interest rates caused the management to press for a reduction in stocks to earn more interest. Rapid inflation had been another factor justifying some slack in stock levels. Finally although the volume of sales had been maintained, trading was tougher as costs had gone on rising.

Buyers were made aware of the potential interest which could be earned by reducing stocks, though interest was not charged to subsidiaries.

22. The company reduced its stocks by nearly 15 per cent. The VAT increase in June 1979 led to disruption and a fall in demand. After discussions with leading industrialists, the Chairman took a pessimistic view of the economy, and in the autumn of 1979 made a policy decision to cut stocks. The company operated in financial markets as well as retailing and so the management were more aware than others of the very profitable opportunities for switching resources from stocks to the financial markets.

In the event stocks were reduced more than sales which fell less than was expected. Consequently there was some deterioration in services to customers, and so the company increased stocks in the following year.

23. The company reduced its stocks by nearly ten per cent. The reduction in stocks was not caused by the recession or the financial squeeze. The company was efficient, profitable and cash rich. At the end of 1979 the company had been over stocked. It had built up stocks of a fashion that had not sold as well as expected, and it had increased stocks to intensify

its competitiveness. At the end of 1980 these special factors did not apply. The company did not increase stocks for tax purposes. Tax relief was available elsewhere in the group.

24. The company cut its stocks by a quarter. The recession slashed profits. The pressure on the company to reduce stocks started in July 1979. The decision coincided with the appointment of a new managing director who adopted a new strategy. In the past the company had taken advantage of opportunities to borrow. In future it would generate cash. Also a period of high interest rates, recession and slow trade was foreseen. The company sold off one business and closed shops and factories. The elimination of stocks of those operations accounted for most of the reduction in stocks.

25. The directors of the company aimed to limit its gearing ratio to 30 per cent. A set-back in business squeezed profits and put pressure on gearing. From the autumn of 1979 the management planned to reduce stocks. Also there was considerable slack in stock levels. For a part of the business the rate of stock turnover was less than twice a year. The company had bought ahead in another part of the business to take advantage of tax relief on stocks. The elimination of these tax stocks accounted for more than a quarter of the reduction in stocks of nearly twenty per cent.

26. Stocks were cut by 13 per cent. The stocks to sales ratio had risen between 1976 and 1979. The recession and high interest rates caused a fall in profits and the management decided to reduce stocks. A manager was appointed to a new post, controller of stocks. He had to initial all new orders. The measures taken to reduce stocks included directions to store managers to cut the period of sales covered by stocks and orders from ten to eight weeks, direct deliveries to shops were controlled more closely, the range of lines and pack sizes was cut and a switch towards home produced goods and away from imports resulted in some saving of stocks.

The company planned to raise its stock turnover from three in 1979/80 to 4.5 in 1984/85, but expected stocks to rise a little in volume terms in 1981/82 and the stocks to sales ratio to fall slightly.

27. The company reduced its stocks in money terms by more than thirty per cent. Sales fell by 15 per cent between the first half of 1980 and the first half of 1981. The other factor contributing to the reduction of stocks was the introduction of computer stock control.

28. Stocks were reduced by nearly 15 per cent. The VAT increase in 1979 had to the management's surprise, little impact on business in July and August. But sales fell away in September and October. This fall was at first attributed to the engineering strike but business did not recover. So stocks at the end of 1979 were much higher than intended. In 1980 the management reacted to the events of 1979 and cut stocks.

Stock control started with an estimate of total sales, but an estimate of stocks was also built up product by product. In 1980 the estimate for total stocks was imposed on the aggregate of the estimates for products. An example of the measures taken to reduce stocks was to cover 40 per cent rather than 50 per cent of expected requirements. The company took greater risks with meeting orders by obtaining goods from suppliers instead of holding stocks.

DISTRIBUTORS

29. The company's main business was distribution of motor vehicles. Stocks were reduced by 18 per cent. The sales estimates for the following half year showed an increase in sales but these estimates were made by the operating units and were treated with scepticism at the head office. The causes of destocking were an overstocked position at the beginning of the year when the fall off in trade was not recognised, and high interest rates. An unusual feature of the business was that manufacturers could, to a degree, force stocks on to the tied distributor. For example, they could agree to the delivery of a product the customer required only on condition that he accepted other products.

30. The main reasons for the 14 per cent fall in stocks were the fall in demand which was rather faster than the fall in stocks, and the change in tax rules for stocks. The destocking was uneven across subsidiaries. Stocks had got out of control during a period of rapid expansion at one subsidiary which lost the UK franchise for a product line during the year. Another subsidiary had a fire which reduced stocks. The financial squeeze was not an important factor.

31. The company reduced its stocks by 29 per cent. The main reason for destocking was the change in the tax rules for stock relief. The company had stocked up at previous year ends by bringing forward purchases from the following year. Removal of the tax incentive to hold stocks meant there was no reason left to hold large stocks. The financial squeeze was not a factor.

32. The company reduced stocks by more than twenty per cent. Two thirds of the fall was a reduction of stocks at sea brought about by a switch to using North Sea oil in place of imported oil, and the absence of precautionary and speculative buying (to protect against interruption of supplies and in advance of expected price rises) at the end of 1980. Also demand had fallen by roughly twenty per cent between the end of 1979 and the end of 1980 and the company, which was a subsidiary of an international company, was committed to providing a cash flow by destocking in the corporate plan for 1980.

33. The company reduced stocks by 31 per cent. One division held a franchise for the sale in the UK and Belgium of products made in the UK by an American based company. In 1980 friction between the two companies built up, perhaps because the American company was under pressure from the recession. The companies decided to end the franchise agreement, so the distributor ran down and sold off stocks of the franchise products. At the year end the company was negotiating to franchise the products of an overseas manufacturer. Apart from this major cause of destocking, the reduction in stocks at other divisions was not planned or attributable to the financial squeeze, decline in demand or changes in tax rules.